Surviving
DEPRESSION

A Catholic Approach

Surviving DEPRESSION

A Catholic Approach

By
Kathryn James Hermes, fsp

Pauline
BOOKS & MEDIA
Boston

Library of Congress Cataloging-in-Publication Data

Hermes, Kathryn.

  Surviving depression: a Catholic approach / by Kathryn J. Hermes.

    p. cm.

Includes bibliographical references.

  ISBN 0-8198-7077-3

  1. Depressed persons—Religious life. 2. Depression,

Mental—Religious aspects—Catholic Church. I. Title.

  BV4910.34.H47 2004

  248.8'625—dc22

                               2003020925

Published in the U.S.A. by Pauline Books & Media, 50 Saint Pauls Avenue, Boston, MA 02130-3491.

Printed in the U.S.A.

www.pauline.org

Pauline Books & Media is the publishing house of the Daughters of St. Paul, an international congregation of women religious serving the Church with the communications media.

5 6 7 8 9 10   12 11 10 09 08

*I am grateful to all those
who have trusted me with their story.*

Contents

Introduction

Depression Has Many Faces

If you have picked up this book, you are most likely wondering if "surviving" depression is possible for you or someone you know. Perhaps you are grasping at one more glimmer of hope that your or another's depression might be lifted. It is estimated that 35 to 40 million Americans living today will suffer from major depression at some time during their lives, with about half of this amount suffering from symptoms of recurring depression. Despite the number of people who have been depressed, are depressed, or know someone who is depressed, there is an amazing lack of understanding about depression.

I am not a psychologist. I am not a theologian. My claim to credibility in writing *Surviving Depression: A Catholic Approach* is that I have been seriously depressed and have spent a lot of time struggling with God in my depression. I know depression from the inside. I know the spiritual anguish it brings. I know the loneliness, the isolation, the fear of "losing it," and I believe one truly understands depression not by studying or reading about it, but by living with it.

In June of 1985, I was admitted to St. Elizabeth's Hospital in Brighton, Massachusetts for simple outpatient surgery. I went into the surgery a healthy, strong, ambitious, and articulate young woman of twenty-one. I came out of the recovery unit with something terribly wrong. Four days later, I was told that I had had a stroke. I was paralyzed on my right side. I couldn't stand up. I had no strength. I had lost much of my memory. I couldn't use even the most basic vocabulary. Two weeks and many tests later, I was released from the hospital and began a long journey of rehabilitation.

Though I recovered much of my strength and coordination within the first few years, for the following twelve years I seemed unable to regain my emotional stability. I quickly found myself in a manic-depressive cycle that became increasingly more pronounced. Violent mood swings sent me crashing between effervescent periods of incredible activity and black nights of paralyzing depression. It was only twelve years after my stroke that I would be diagnosed with Temporal Lobe Epilepsy (TLE), a bipolar organic disorder—which brought about another cycle of depression as I began to live with a new "label."

God Has Many Faces

During those first weeks after the stroke, I clearly remember thinking: God has given me this stroke and I will accept it with graciousness. This is the will of God and God certainly has some reason for it. And I accepted it with peace...or so I thought. It took six years for me to realize how angry I was—angry at God, angry at everyone around me, angry at the world. At that time, I began regular spiritual direction. The more I shared what was in my heart, the angrier I became, and the farther away God seemed. I could not understand what possible meaning the cross could have. I spent a year unable to believe God even existed. In this spiritual "blackout," I read over and over again the second part of the book of Isaiah, though the words were like sandpaper to my heart:

> O afflicted one, storm-tossed, and not comforted
> look, I am about to set your stones in antimony,
> lay your foundations with sapphires.
> I will make your pinnacles of rubies,
> your gates of jewels, and your wall of precious
>   stones (54:11–12).

As the cycle of depressions came and went, with confusion and despair clouding my vision, I wrestled with God, trying to understand just one question: *Why me?!* Though I never received an answer to that question, was never given a clue to understanding the meaning of my suffering, I was gradually—*very gradually*—able to realize that it was no longer an issue for me. I didn't need an answer; I could live with the mystery.

Depression spares no one. Christians become as depressed as anyone else does; priests, and men and women religious suffer from depression. Teens in the flower of youthful dreams become depressed. Even children can become depressed. It might seem that people who have faith or a future should have no reason to be depressed. They should be able to pray, dream, or will themselves out of it. It is hard to reconcile what many still incorrectly see as a moral deficiency with faith in the power of God. However, depression is just an expression of our fragile human vulnerability. Ironically, this empty darkness is often the source of immense creativity, the black night that gently announces the advent of the divine.

Into this book are woven many individuals' unique experiences of depression. As you read these pages, you may find characteristics or details that hit home, that mesh with your own experience. People who have suffered depression can learn so much from each other's stories. Nevertheless, not every experience related here will be completely like yours. You may feel more or less depressed than people in the stories I have included. You may or may not experience the symptoms narrated here. Be aware, therefore, that flashes of insight or recognition are not a replacement for accurate diagnosis. This book is not intended for self-diagnosis and does not address the more critical needs of those who suffer severe or psychotic cases of depression or bipolar disorder. Rather, it is meant to be a companion for you as you, or a friend of yours, struggles with his or her dark phases of life. Much in our Catholic tradition and in spirituality can offer strength, comfort, and powerful insight into this struggle. These pages will introduce you to this wealth and be with you as you find God in new ways along this part of your life's journey.

❦❦❦❦❦

Ah to tear away once and for all—
to rip my heart out of my breast
and toss to the stars....
This heart so dark and full of
sadness—
this heart so full of alienating pain—
this heart alone against so many feelings—
corrupted by dreams and imaginings—
forsaken by promise and tender words.
So slowly turned to stone...
and now this quaking—
the urge to break forth...
to soar to the heavens and freedom.
And where will "i" be when
you take sudden flight—
will you take me with you
on your wings of pearl?

Sr. Thomas Halpin, FSP
April 24, 1994

_ꕷ 1 ꕷ_

What Does Depression Look Like?

"I don't want anyone to know I feel this bad, but sometimes I don't even want to get out of bed." *Cheyanne*

———————

"When I was depressed I felt like a non-person, a burden. The darkness engulfed and suffocated everything. Certain few "true" friends who knew and loved me threw out lifelines that I was able to grab hold of. I still prayed even though it seemed useless, but one day Jesus' message shouted through the weltering gloom that he too had experienced the same darkness on the cross. Those last moments were actually the depth of darkness for him, feeling even his Father disowned him. As hard as I tried, I couldn't find life in this inspiration. I couldn't believe that his situation could touch mine. I shared this with a friend and her response was one of those lifelines: 'Well, if you can't believe right now, let me believe for you. Put your trust in my belief that it is true.' " *Anne*

———————

"Depression was a swirling black hole that sucked me in until I was in well over my head and drowning," a friend shared with me. "The energy to fight against it was immense and at times I just let it take over. I was so tired." Everyone who has suffered from depression has their own images of the period of their life dominated by this illness. Depression is a medical condition that can be accompanied by panic attacks, anxiety, sadness, suicidal thoughts, feelings of despair and helplessness, and a sense of being overwhelmed.

Depression plays hide and seek with its victims. Those closest to the depressed person often see it first. They might notice a certain lethargy in their friend, or be surprised by an uncharacteristic display of anxiety. Friends and family members may grow tired of the sufferer's overbearing sadness or negative thinking.

Depression usually carries the stigma of failure. The suggestion by others that one might be feeling depressed is often perceived as an "accusation," a statement about one's inner weakness. "I am not depressed, I'm just down," a depressed person states, with a stiff upper lip. "I have nothing to be depressed about. How could I have depression?" The person suffering from depression may actually believe that he or she is not depressed. It is hidden from him or herself most of all.

How Do I Know If I Am Depressed?

There are many different "levels" of depression. Feeling blue, temporary malaise, or the sadness that accompanies grieving may temporarily disrupt our normal patterns of life. When the change of mood outlives the event that triggered the "moodiness," however, it can become a serious liability to healthy emotional living. When the depressed mood lingers on and one's interest in life diminishes, a person's serious attention to their psychic and emotional life will give them the best chance at resuming their life.

But sometimes it's hard to tell if what one is feeling is, in fact, depression. Through the years, I have picked up books on depression with the secret thought: *maybe this book will convince me that I really am depressed. Then I will at least know that I am not crazy....* At other times I didn't want information, hoping that the dark feelings inside would keep out of sight long enough so that I could fool myself into thinking everything was going to be okay. Some days I wanted to be able to name and understand the terrible feelings within me, other days I wanted to convince myself they weren't there. People suffering from depression often swing back and forth between being sure they are depressed to being certain they *aren't*, between wanting to know the truth and *not* wanting to. How do you know if what you're feeling is depression? To begin with, you might ask yourself the following questions:

> Have I become moody, or do I have a significantly strong melancholic mood most of the day, every day?
>
> Have I lost interest in people and activities?
>
> Have I gained or lost a significant amount of weight in the recent past?

Do I have problems falling asleep, or do I wake unbearably early?

Do I find that all my thinking is concentrated on surviving the day at hand or with wondering what is wrong with me?

Do I feel tired all day?

Do I feel like doing nothing?

Do I feel little or no energy?

Do I use drugs, alcohol, pornography, sex, or any other addictive behavior to avoid dealing with reality or to escape my emotions?

Do I have trouble concentrating?

Do I see only bad things when I look at myself?

Do I have recurring thoughts of death and suicide?

Do I feel abnormally restless?

Do I cry a lot?

Where Does Depression Come From?

Biological causes account for a large percentage of the cases of depression. Emotional stability is closely related to the normal formation and function of a number of vital chemicals that exist in the brain called neurotransmitters. Neurotransmitters are the chemical messengers that enable nerve cells (neurons) to communicate. Neurotransmitters are released into the gaps between nerve cells to help nerve messages flow from one cell to another. Insufficient production of neurotransmitters means that the nerve messages crucial for the stimulation of areas of the brain are not communicated. Alterations in neurotransmission in areas of the brain that control mood and emotion may result in depression.

Specific diseases can cause depression by affecting neurotransmitter production. Diseases of the central nervous system, as well as infectious diseases, diseases of the immune system, and nutritional deficiencies can affect brain chemistry. An imbalance of various hormones can cause depression. Depression can cripple women during menopause. Genetic factors may also be indicated as the cause of depression. Recent studies have shown that individuals with a short version of a particular gene involved in the production of a key brain chemical are more than twice as likely to get depressed.

Besides physical causes, there are psychological causes for depression as well. Stress is a significant psychological cause. Today's "information overload" is a primary cause of stress and depression. Technology delivers information at a pace that is simply too much for a person to reasonably handle. People are finding it increasingly difficult to deal with their e-mail, their instant messages and voicemail, their beepers and PDA's, their faxes and FedEx's, and the constant demand of having to understand a technology that seemingly changes every day, while at the same time produce quality work at a faster rate. Where before a business might have had to compete with another across town, today businesses compete with the whole world via internet. The stress of not being able to keep up makes people vulnerable to depression.

Events such as the loss of a job, the death of a loved one, the loss of a good friend, financial difficulties, a move, or change of school are also very stressful events. The losses we experience in life can be contributing factors to depression. A study carried out at the University of Oregon and the University of Pittsburgh concluded that statistically stressful life-events often precede depression. Prolonged or acute stress and the over-secretion of stress hormones may impair regions of the brain believed to be involved in maintaining mood.

> *"Depression, like the common cold, is no respecter of persons."*
> Myra Chave-Jones,
> *Coping with Depression*

Recent studies have indicated that humiliation may also trigger depression, even more than personal losses. The death of a family member or a friend is sad, but such events do not affect an individual's personal identity as much as the humiliation that results from losing a job, working under an employer who belittles your work, or being shamed throughout your career.

Fifty percent of all people who suffer Post-Traumatic Stress Disorder, or PTSD, also suffer from depression. Post-Traumatic Stress Disorder can occur following the experience or witnessing of life-threatening events such as military combat, natural disasters, terrorist incidents, serious accidents, or violent personal assaults like rape. Depression is associated with PTSD, and symptoms can be severe enough to impair the person's daily life.

Personal views we hold about ourselves can also trigger depression. Idealistic people are a gift to the human race. Their ideals and values articulate for the rest of us what we can become. Idealistic people, however, can set themselves up for depression: first, they may never seem able to reach their own ideals—and neither can anyone else—resulting in cynicism and depression; second, idealistic people may actually achieve the ideals they have set for themselves, only to find that they must immediately set new and higher ideals to reach. Life becomes an endless chase after utopian dreams.

Because of our high ideals, Christians are sometimes prime targets for depression. High expectations about how to live reinforce ideals that can be unrealistic: *Christians never get angry. Christians never get divorced. Christian families don't have problems. God only loves Christians who are perfect.* If we just had enough faith, we wouldn't need antidepressant medication. If we believed in the power of prayer, wouldn't we be happy? If Christians really believed in God, shouldn't we be able to "play the part" of a person of faith? "Playing parts" is a piece of the problem in which a Christian, or any person of high standards, can find themselves. We imagine what the ideal Christian should be and realize that *we're not it.* But we pretend that we are, sometimes at least. But eventually the knocks of life break this false image of ourselves and we discover that we aren't what "Christians should be." The tyranny of the image of the perfect Christian leads to its own type of depression, a depression that swirls around the fear that God doesn't love those who don't live up to "my"—not God's—expectations. By confusing God's expectations with our own, we are led to a sense of failure and defeatism. *We* expect perfection of ourselves ("God, I thank you that I am not greedy, dishonest, and unfaithful in marriage, like other people," cf. Lk 18:11). God, instead, extends the gift of reconciliation.

Finally, the misunderstanding of others accentuates depression. No one with any sensitivity would expect a person with a broken leg to run a mile or carry a fifty-pound package. It's more difficult, however, to understand and be sensitive to a person who is depressed. People suffering from depression may be afraid to admit they are feeling so low. Admitting this and pursuing counseling or medication would not only expose them to the stigma associated with depression or mental illness, it could also lead to isolation, possible job loss, and family misunderstanding. Often people suffering from depression remain locked in their fears, alone with their anxieties, pretending to be powerful, all the time wishing they could share with someone how badly they feel.

Depression is a complex illness probably best explained not by genes or circumstances alone, but by the interaction of the two.

Jesus Made Tears Sacred

Persons suffering from depression experience their own vulnerability in a particularly profound way: an experience no one likes, but everyone needs. Jesus made himself vulnerable. He shed tears in his life, died as a seeming failure, left this earth with only a handful of followers who had earlier deserted him. As he hung on the cross, he had only his trust in his Father, the one possession of which nothing could deprive him. Jesus made tears sacred, because he cried. He knew the agony and the frustration of our problems. He chose to bear all that is human, and to bring it with him on his return to the Father. The One who sits at God's right hand knows what it is to cry. He preached an upside-down world in which the poor, the marginalized, the suffering, those who agonize through emotional pain, are the first, the guests of honor, and the privileged.

The vulnerability of depression doesn't feel holy. It feels like hell. There seems to be no light toward which to walk. There seem to be no options. There often seems no reason to live. Few experiences expose to us our vulnerability in such a sharp way.

In the winter of 1829, Francis Libermann, a young seminarian studying at St. Sulpice in Paris, began experiencing excessive fatigue. It became more and more difficult to handle his emotions. Assuming that his studies in theology were wearing him out, he followed his doctor's advice and began to absent himself from his classes in order to take extra time to rest. As the weeks wore on, however, Libermann began to feel increasingly uneasy, as he had a foreboding that there was something seriously wrong with his health. One day, while visiting another seminarian in the infirmary, a wild shock ripped through his body. Francis fell to the ground in an epileptic fit. When he awoke several hours later, lying on an infirmary bed, Francis felt as if someone had beaten him with clubs. His head throbbed and his eyes were unable to focus. Accustomed as he was to turning to Jesus as his model for life, Francis turned to the Lord to whom he had given his life and prayed, "It is well, O Lord, that you have permitted me to be subject to all this. I am in the midst of torment, but I will not yield to despair."

When the doctor visited Francis, he was surprised to see the young man serene and smiling. Epileptic attacks usually leave their victims feeling gloomy, depressed, and hypersensitive, but the doctor was amazed that the young seminarian exhibited none of these emotional states. Shortly after the doctor left his patient, however, anxiety began to creep into Libermann's thoughts. Panic over whether his condition would force him to give up his dream to be ordained a priest rolled into feelings of morbid guilt and fear that this illness was God's punishment for something he had done. Such floundering back and forth between peace and despair became all-too-familiar to Francis, whose battle with depression lasted the rest of his life.

> *"Remember, you are held safe. You are loved. You are protected."*
> Henri Nouwen,
> *The Inner Voice of Love*

With time, the epileptic seizures increased. Libermann began to call his mysterious torment "my beloved malady." When he felt engulfed by depression, Francis turned to the chapel or hid in his room, kneeling in prayer, waiting for the black clouds to scatter. He counteracted the anxiety that accompanied the onset of his seizures with a peaceful abandonment to the love of God. Though Francis determined to accept this turn in his health with trust and a peaceful love, the undercurrent in the ocean of his moods was one of loneliness, failure, and discouragement. The depression often tempted him to throw himself off a bridge into the Seine River. The dark waters seemed to call to him to finally be done with the misery of his life. The temptation was strong, almost irresistible, and he would have to hurry across the bridge, lest he gave in to the siren call of the waters that seemed to promise peace. Francis Libermann once confessed that he never crossed a bridge without the urge to cast himself into the waters below. The uncontrollable urge to end his miserable life was so strong that even in his room he never kept a knife or sharp object within reach.

Eventually his superiors reluctantly dismissed Libermann from the seminary. Francis's suffering, however, made him a master at understanding the struggles and sufferings of others. Gradually, seminarians began coming to him for spiritual guidance, and he became the novice master of the ecclesiastical Society of Jesus and Mary, more commonly known as the Spiritans, founded by John Eudes for the education of priests for the missions. In time, Libermann would gather a group of individuals together to form a small religious community to minister to newly freed slaves in Haiti, Reunion, and Mauritius.

Francis Libermann traveled to Rome in 1838 to request permission to form and direct this new congregation. While there, he had an audience with Pope Gregory XVI, who, upon blessing him, uttered the prophetic words, "*Sará un santo* (he will be a saint)." With Vatican approval, the new congregation was begun, and on Pentecost, 1841, Libermann was finally ordained a priest.

Insist on God's Love for You

Throughout Libermann's life, it was his personal experience of suffering, beginning from his youth, that had made him a gentle and insightful assistant to those who suffered. Today he is known as Venerable Francis Libermann, meaning that the Church has recognized the heroism of his virtues. Though Francis's sufferings were with him until the day he died, he often prayed:

> *O most holy and adorable Spirit of my Jesus, let me hear your gentle voice. Refresh me with your precious inspiration. O divine Spirit, I want to be before you like a light feather, so that your breath may carry me where it will, and that I may not offer the least resistance to it.*

Libermann had learned that every experience in life, even the most discouraging and defeating, can be the breath of the Spirit because our sufferings do not define who we are. Despite the shroud depression spins around our life, it does *not* define who we are. As Pope John Paul II has often said in speaking to the sick and infirm, "God chooses the fragile and weak to manifest his divine power to those who trust him, especially in moments when all seems lost." Francis Libermann is especially suited as a guide for those who suffer depression. His unflagging insistence on God's love for him gave him the courage to turn his life over to the guidance of the Spirit, who always opens the door to hope.

Suggestion for prayer

Pray the first sorrowful mystery of the Rosary, the Agony of Jesus in the Garden. Pray this decade of the Rosary gently—one Our Father and ten Hail Marys—and give yourself a chance to stay with Jesus in his sorrow and tears. Enter into Jesus and see, from the inside, what he is feeling as he prays to his Father for help. Then allow Jesus to feel, from the inside, what you are feeling. Listen to what Jesus has to say to you.

ᘓ ✿ ᘔ

For one who is depressed

- Make a chart of the factors that could be important to understanding your depression.
- Start to write your own story. Note major events, prayer experiences, dreams, inspirations, sudden turns in the road, surprising discoveries you had never expected.

For a friend

Set aside a few hours every other week just to visit with someone who is depressed. Provide a welcome distraction by bringing over your pet if you have one. Listen and show your understanding. Invite your friend to a movie, take him or her out for ice cream, or go for a walk together.

Some Symptoms of Depression

- crying

- anger

- weight loss or gain

- fear and anxiety

- violent mood swings

- withdrawal

- irritability

- hopelessness

- feeling of guilt

- oversensitivity

- bursting into tears

- feelings of inadequacy

- change of sleep patterns

- uncontrollable feelings of despair

- no interest in food, or unusual overeating

- apathy

- feeling worthless

- lacking all motivation

- sense of futility

_ ⸙ 2 ⸙ _

"If Only You Tried Harder"

"I don't know why I want to cry. When my friends and I go out to dinner sometimes I tell them how I am feeling. As soon as I start, they say, 'Do we have to listen to that again? Get over it. Everybody has something to deal with.' I just want someone to listen to me." *Cherrie*

"One day a friend said to me, 'You need help; you are depressed.' I will always be grateful to her. I didn't realize I was depressed. Actually, I did not even realize how much I was suffering. I thought everyone felt the way I did. She has continued to be a friend and to stand by me during these years of healing." *Marie*

Just about every depressed person has heard one form or other of these words:

"Everybody has a rainy day."

"Look on the bright side."

"Pull yourself up by your bootstraps."

"That's the way the ball bounces."

"You'll get over it."

"If only you tried harder."

"Just stop and smell the roses."

"It can't be *that* bad."

At a certain point, those who suffer from depression may feel that people must be thinking these things even if they don't say them. "Maybe they're right. I'm just looking at the dark side of things. If I really wanted to, I'd just shake myself out of this." But at other times these clichés spark anger.

"If only I *could* snap out of this!"

"Yes, it *is* this bad!"

"No! There *are* no roses to smell!"

"For your information, *I didn't stand in line for this!*"

While the depressed person may feel like shouting these words at those who respond insensitively to their sadness, somewhere deep down inside there is a fear that what people say is in fact true. "If I just tried harder, maybe I could beat this." The fact remains, however, that you *can't* beat depression by willing it away. Depression, like any other medical condition, needs to be addressed seriously. It needs to be dealt with head on. Admitting you have depression is not an expression of defeat. *Not* admitting it is.

When a person is depressed, he or she just wants someone to listen to what is hurting inside. We want someone to see the tears we may not be shedding, but long to have wiped away. A black tunnel closes in, snuffing out any flicker of light, and often the only thing a depressed person has left to talk about is the dark tunnel itself. Depression can be so debilitating that it takes up all of a person's attention and energy.

Conversations that center almost exclusively on one's problems, however, soon turn people off. Friends stop calling. When people want a good time, inviting someone who is depressed takes too much emotional energy. Little by little, the person suffering from depression finds him or herself isolated from others. Friendships imperceptibly unravel as the depressed person retreats into a world that becomes daily more incomprehensible and hopeless. Isolation, a low sense of self-worth, and fear of abandonment throw cold water on any attempts to start new friendships or revive old ones. Friendship may even hold no attraction at all; energy for reaching out to others just isn't there. Friendships built on attraction and shared synergy may seem cruelly out of reach.

Christ Redefined Friendship

The life, death, and resurrection of Jesus, however, have redefined friendship. For Christians, friendship is no longer defined by mere attraction and what another person can do for us, but by the gift of self to others, because this is what Jesus did. In Christ Jesus, Christians have been called to live and worship God *in community.* The Christian community is a model of the loveliness of being chosen to be intimate friends with the Lord and each other: friendships that are "lovely" because they are received and mutually worked at. In the Christian community, the rich live and worship with the poor, the computer geek with the second grader, the sophisticated with the simple, and the CEO with the mechanic. The Christian community is realized when individuals embody the new potential for human nature and the possibility of graced community with others which Christ has made possible. Christians are called into a community of persons gathered together not by attraction, but by a call in Christ Jesus, through the power of his Spirit, for the glory of the Father.

Creating a Supportive Network of Friends

"Having someone to talk to on a regular basis is very helpful," Karl believes. "You know they are always there 'just in case' you're really desperate some day and need some help quick!" If you are suffering with depression, friendships may be difficult to cultivate, but they are essential for healing. Start by finding at least five people you can call on when you need someone to talk to—people who can count on you for friendship as well. In looking for people who will be part of this support network, seek persons who can empathize with you and listen, people who can affirm your individuality and your strengths, and treat you with love, humor, and honesty. Make sure that in your support network, you choose one or two people who could take you out for fun activities when you need a good laugh to shake away the darkness. People in your support network should be open-minded and comfortable when you describe how you are feeling and what you want. You will want the kind of person who can accept your ups and downs without being judgmental. Relatives, spouses, soul-friends, therapists, counselors, members of your parish or church community, and neighbors can all be a part of this support network.

After forming a support network, it's a good idea to clarify for yourself how you want others to treat you—and *not* treat you—when you're feeling depressed (or manic). An honest talk with each person about the type of support you need should include freedom for the other person to reflect on whether or not she or he feels able to be there for you in the way you have described. Also, ask questions about *their* preferences. Discuss when they would find it easiest for you to contact them. What things do they like to do? When during the week are they most available to go out for a cup of coffee or a movie? Try to harmonize as much as possible their preferences with your needs. Depending on each person's gifts and personality, you might contact one when you need to talk for a few moments on the phone,

"Maybe I'm not making big changes in the world, but if I have somehow helped or encouraged somebody along the journey, then I've done what I'm called to do."
Sister Thea Bowman

another when you would like to check out your judgment before making a decision, a third if you need to hand over important decisions for a short period of time, or any of them if you just want someone who can make you laugh.

Perhaps one of your support friends would be willing to give you a ride to Mass on Sunday or pray with you over the phone. Using guided imagery meditations over the phone are especially effective. I have prayed with friends when they have called and were especially down or felt they were spinning out of control. As we pray together, we picture Jesus in our imaginations. Then I guide them to speak with him and to hand over to him the bundle of their fears or emotional pain. Sometimes I suggest words they can say to Jesus, and often they end up speaking spontaneously to him while we are praying. I conclude by asking them what Jesus is saying to them in response. This sharing in another person's encounter with the Lord is a privileged moment. As I have prayed with others, I have sensed how Jesus calms them, allowing his love to gently heal their worries and fears.

As these relationships of self-gift and availability grow, you will discover little things about the people in your support group. When you're able, send a card on a person's birthday or a holiday. Drop off a special dessert—even if you buy it instead of cooking it yourself. Try to discover the things they like to do and, when you get together, suggest doing those things first. Notice when they may feel stressed and offer to treat them to coffee, to walk their dog, or e-mail them a message.

Sacrificial Giving and Grateful Receiving

Friendship made a life-changing difference to forty-five-year-old Gail, who lives in Virginia. She was diagnosed with manic depression when she was nineteen. Gail responded well to her treatment and was able to lead a productive life. However, ten years later a car hit her, and things drastically fell apart. Her mood swings grew more pronounced, and her family felt they could not care for her. "My mother herself was bipolar, so it was difficult for my parents to deal with my situation. I was trying to get a job and living alone," she remembers. "That whole period was a terrible time. The medication I had been on was no longer effective and I even tried to commit suicide." The "miracle" of healing that God worked in her life was the miracle of friendship. "I was pretty desperate," Gail remembers, "so I put an ad in the paper. Think of a huge city newspaper, and one little ad on one page, just three lines long. Imagine someone finding those three lines and calling you up. That's exactly what happened. Ben and I met together and eventually married. To me that's the miracle: God bringing us together. Ben found me and then discovered something in me that he loved. Whether I believed it was possible or not, he did."

Ben remembers the day Gail told him she was bipolar. "I hadn't expected that, but the more I thought about it, the more I realized that it was not a reason to cut off our relationship. By the time we decided to marry, I had accepted that manic depression was a part of her life."

Gail believes that her illness is much easier to cope with because of the love that she has received. "He has been the greatest husband for ten years," she says. "He has provided all the stability I need in my life, all the love I could ever want. In turn I give him emotional support by just being there for him and listening." Helping another person enriches your life in ways no one else sees. "Don't be afraid to develop a relationship with someone who may be suffering from depression," Ben says. "Having a relationship has helped both Gail and me greatly. Being in love with each other, together with each other, has made life more beautiful for both of us."

> *"God bless the poor, God bless the sick, and bless our human race. God bless our food, God bless our drink. All homes, O God, embrace."*
> Saint Brigit of Kildare

Friendships founded on sacrificial giving and grateful receiving—on the part of both persons—increase love in the world. Having a meaning larger than oneself can help a person suffering from depression to take a step toward connection and presence. More often than not, others are just waiting for you to ask them to be a part of your life. In a deeply Christian way, these people become intimate friends because their friendship transcends mutual attraction and interest. We can become a sacrament of Christ's presence for each other, a eucharistic reality through the element of self-gift that characterizes these supportive relationships.

The Liturgy: A School of Remembering God's Faithfulness

The Eucharistic Liturgy brings the depth of the emotion in our lives into contact with the pathos of God. The Liturgy of the Eucharist is the only place that can hold both the tension of sorrow and the exuberance of praise. Sorrow without praise is deadening; praise that does not encounter sorrow is a hollow experience. In the rites and the prayers of the liturgy, in its readings and doxologies, we discover who we are, but also, and primarily, we discover who God is for us. In the reassuring repetition of rites and prayers, we are taught and shaped by the story of God's intervention in our life.

The prefaces and Eucharistic prayers of the Mass in particular are privileged places for this discovery. Each preface recounts the mystery of creation *and* redemption. The preface for Eucharistic Prayer II states that Jesus is the "Word through whom [the Father] made the universe, the savior [he] sent to redeem us," born of Mary through the power of the Spirit. Jesus put an end to death, rose from the dead, and won for God "a holy people," of whom we are a member. In the first preface of Easter, we praise God for sending us his Son, who has become our paschal sacrifice. "He is the true Lamb who took away the sin of the world." The second preface of Easter reminds us that God: "has made us children of the light, rising to new and everlasting life." In the first preface for Ordinary Time, we recall that: "Everywhere we proclaim your mighty works for you have called us *out of darkness into your own wonderful light*." And in the second preface for Christmas, we marvel at the mystery of the Incarnation: "No eye can see his glory as our God, yet now he is seen as one like us.... He has come to lift up all things to himself, to restore unity to creation, and to lead mankind from exile into your heavenly kingdom." As if in wonder before the mystery of darkness, leading to light, we then join the angels and saints in praise of God, singing the *Sanctus*.

Eucharistic Prayer IV recounts God's pursuit of humanity from the moment of creation through the covenants and prophets who taught us to hope and to believe. In the fullness of time, God gave what was most precious to him to be our Savior: the Son he loved as himself. God sent him in love to proclaim the good news, freedom, joy, and, through his obedience and death, he won for us salvation so that we might live for God alone.

In the Liturgy of the Eucharist, the sorrow and pain of disobedience and human vulnerability meet the aching love of a God who will not let his people die. We too are caught up in this eucharistic work of Jesus, the divine Good Samaritan who served his creatures, washed his apostles' feet, and who tends to all our wounds in the liturgy. The relationships you cultivate among the members of your team or with those who share with you the sorrows and struggles of your depression, are just such Good Samaritan relationships, extending the Eucharistic presence of Jesus, Servant and Samaritan, in the world today.

What I receive from the Eucharistic Liturgy doesn't depend on how I feel or whether I have a "good experience" at Mass. Rather, it is about what *God* has done, and all that God promises to do. As Catholics, our daily lives are not fully broken open until joined with others in this art of praising and thanking God in the midst of our human situation. To pray *for* and *with* and *out of* a suffering world, out of our own suffering is to learn something true about praise and blessing; it is to profess most authentically that God is God, the One who alone deserves our worship and adoration. To continue to worship in the liturgy, to acknowledge God in the midst of adversity as well as in good fortune, is to understand ever more deeply who we are in relation to God. The liturgy is best celebrated when we bring real life to the healing and consoling, the reconciling and illuminating work of God. There we learn to speak the language we pray. We are refashioned and our perspectives enlightened through the repeated hymns of praise and thanksgiving, our voices raised with the angels in the proclamation of the power of God's love: *Holy, Holy, Holy Lord, God of power and might.* The liturgy is a school for remembering who God *has* promised to be, and by recalling who God has been for us, we can then recall who God *will* be. And we can remind God to be God—to come and save us *now!*

Suggestion for prayer

Using an old missalette, and in a quiet moment, take a pen and underline in the Order of the Mass the statements about what God has done for us. Circle the words: praise, thanksgiving, and joy. Read some of the Scripture readings and underline the words that express the human situation in all of its drama and complexity. Use this missalette at Mass to enter more deeply into the mystery of the liturgy where God holds and heals us in power and love.

༺ৡ ※ ৡ৸

For one who is depressed

Make a list of five people you could ask to be part of your support team. Write down for yourself what you would like to ask of them.

After contacting these people, begin to network with them, creating a team of people who can offer you assistance and friendship when you need it.

For a friend

Notice if you find yourself using clichés with your friend who suffers from depression. If so, try asking instead, "Can you tell me what it's like for you?" At times, include him or her in your recreational activities.

Suggestions for Support

(Not all of these are helpful or possible for everyone all the time. Choose those best suited for you at this time.)

- Talk with a good friend;

- Reach out to help someone;

- Go to a support group;

- Do a hobby with someone;

- Arrange to be around others;

- Spend time with a pet;

- Go to Mass with a friend;

- Go for a walk with someone;

- Call a crisis clinic or hotline;

- Exercise with someone;

- Join a parish committee with a friend;

- Chat with a family member;

- Spend time with good friends;

- Let yourself be held by someone you love;

- Talk with someone in your parish;

- Pray;

- Choose to be around people who don't criticize, judge, or want to change you, but who accept you for who you are at this point in your life;

- Be okay with who you are, not trying to live up to another's expectations.

⤎ 3 ⤏

"Why Doesn't God Heal Me?"

"I am now the most miserable man living. If what I feel were equally distributed to the whole human family there would be not one cheerful face on earth. Whether I shall ever be better, I cannot tell. I awfully forebode... I shall not. To remain as I am is impossible. I must die or be better it appears to me."
Abraham Lincoln

———

"In the last fifteen years, I have struggled with periods of depression several times. The first time I was seriously depressed, I went for therapy and worked through my memories of trauma and repressed feelings. The second time I became depressed, I was surprised. I thought that I had done that work 'once and for all.' I prayed about this. Actually, I prayed rather desperately. Looking back, I realize that I felt like a failure, as though I did not get it 'right' the first time. God gradually revealed to me that all of this is an important part of my life's spiritual journey. Each time I worked through my issues and my past, it was at a deeper level and I became healthier and more integrated. I became aware that each time I struggled with depression my relationship with God changed. I was able to trust God more. Actually, all of my relationships changed: with myself and with others." *Pat*

———————

Depression affects a person's thoughts, mood, feelings, behavior, and overall health. No scientific terminology can capture the degree of pain experienced by those who suffer from it.

Dreams previously clung to seem to vanish; beauty that once gave inspiration no longer exists. Instead, a person's mind may be filled with negative thoughts such as, "I have failed. I have no value. My views are worthless. All this is my fault. I don't know what is happening to me. Why do I feel this way? I've asked God to help me. Why doesn't he *do* something?"

Jeanne, a friend, once shared with me her struggle with God's presence in her early traumatic experiences. "One day when I was talking to God about the time that I had been sexually abused, I angrily cried out to Jesus, 'Where were you when he did this to me?' In my heart, I heard Jesus respond, 'I was with you, crying.' As I continued in prayer, I understood that Jesus had been there with me during the abuse, and that he had hated to see me hurt. But I also understood that he continued to be with me as I worked through the memories, enlightening me, strengthening me, giving me courage, and healing me."

Those of us who struggle with depression usually wonder why God doesn't do something to help us. Praying for a miracle is often our last hope for help. Since we feel we can't do anything ourselves, we hope that God can. When God doesn't work the expected miracle, we wonder if God cares about us. Or perhaps we think God is punishing us for past failures. But God doesn't usually deal with us by arresting the forces of nature. When a physical miracle is *all* we're hoping for, God can seem to be uninterested in our plight or to have decided that for some mysterious reason we should suffer.

Leaving Behind My Attempts to Fix Depression

In my own experience of depression, I had to learn to acknowledge my helplessness. All my attempts to fix my depression were just that—*my* attempts. I had managed to "surmount" my own struggle with depression through concepts, intellectualization, and learning as much as I could. I understood the causes of my depression, and with the strength of my mind, I moved on. I knew how it was tearing my life apart. I figured out what I needed to do to get better. I became an expert at analyzing defense mechanisms. I set about doing everything I was supposed to do. Yes, *I* did it. Everything should have worked. And it did! Well, it did and it *didn't*. It was as if I needed surgery, but all I could do on my own, without a surgeon, was to take medicine and vitamins. The medicine and the vitamins definitely helped. For seventeen years, they made my life more manageable and calm. But without surgery, I was still on the level of coping. In reality, I needed not just any surgeon, I needed the Divine Surgeon. I needed a miracle.

And over several days of prayer, the Divine Surgeon took me under his care. It was an annual retreat, a full eight days set aside exclusively for prayer. Immediately, upon beginning the retreat, I found myself desiring to contemplate the passion, death, and resurrection of Jesus in the Gospel of John (chapters 18–21). The scene came alive in my imagination and my heart. I saw Jesus standing before Pontius Pilate and his accusers. *How could Jesus stand there while everyone called for his death,* I wondered. *How could he be so calm?* As I placed myself completely into that scene, feeling Jesus' calmness, I began to hear Jesus saying quietly to the crowd, "Yes. Take me. Do what you want with me, for my death will be your salvation." I could see the Father hugging him tightly. "Give yourself over to them," God told his Son. "I can never let you go, no matter what happens. I am with you. You are safe in my arms." After a long period of prayer, I realized that the Father was within me as he was within Jesus. He was also holding me: "Do not be afraid. You are safe in my arms."

"My tears have been my food day and night."

Psalm 42:3

On another day, I contemplated Jesus right after Pilate had condemned him to death and washed his hands of the whole affair. I saw Jesus dragged off by those who had wanted him dead. The moment of terror I felt, as his final walk through Jerusalem began, was excruciating. I prayed many hours, holding that terror in my heart, desiring to comfort Jesus, to tell him I was there for him and that I would not leave him alone.

One day in prayer, I stood beneath the cross and sank to the ground at its foot after he had died. I had told Jesus I would not leave him alone, and so I stayed there keeping watch. I kept the cross before my eyes for hours, feeling the sorrow Mary must have felt, as I asked for the courage to stay near the cross. It was at this point my retreat director pointed out to me that perhaps God was bringing together Jesus' experience and my own. I began to cry when I returned to prayer. For several hours, in prayer before the Eucharist, scenes of my hospital stay after my stroke so many years before alternated with scenes of Jesus' passion and death. It was like watching a movie. My moments of loneliness and fear alternated with Jesus' loneliness and fear. I cried inconsolably for hours—seventeen years worth of tears. God truly was embracing me tightly and saying, "Do not be afraid even of this. I am holding you tightly and nothing can hurt you."

These cleansing tears began a process of healing, a miracle of God's love for me as I began to pray over my "passion." Just as I, in that prayer, had remained beneath the cross after Jesus had died, I now saw Jesus sitting on the floor at the foot of my hospital bed keeping *me* company. As I had stayed with Jesus, he now kept watch with me. The many lonely years of struggling with the consequences of my stroke and the resulting bipolar disorder were "healed" in this prayer. God did not miraculously heal me of Temporal Lobe Epilepsy. Instead, I began to see that though I had kept myself at a sufficient distance from God to protect myself from anything else God could "do" to me, God nevertheless had waited until the right moment to "seize me by the arms" and turn me toward him. I did not receive the miraculous healing I had wanted. I received something better.

God never promised that we would live free from all suffering. God promised that nothing could ever remove us from his love and care, or, as a doctor once put it, "Don't be afraid of the worst that could happen to you. It will, *but it doesn't matter!*" While I couldn't put into words what I felt the first time I heard those words, I instinctively knew them to be true.

A Sacrament of Healing

Although not a prolonged experience like a retreat, the sacrament of Reconciliation is a privileged and easily accessible place to encounter the same healing of Jesus. At the mention of confession, it is unfortunate that sometimes what come to mind are unpleasant images. *Besides,* you might object, *what does confessing our sins to a priest have to do with depression? I need a therapist, not a priest!*

Therapists are indeed wonderful assets on the road to health, and sometimes they are indispensable. Sharing your experience of depression with a friend is helpful. But the sacrament of Reconciliation offers a particular space of encounter with God and with ourselves that cannot be duplicated elsewhere.

When people think of the sacrament of Reconciliation, many think of the shame of "listing their sins" before another person. I suggest, however, that in the sacrament of Reconciliation, Jesus enters into our chaos with love. Rather than lists of sins, it is precisely our chaos that we need to bring to Jesus in this Sacrament. The confusion, overbearing sadness, frustration, guilt, sense of loss that accompany depression can skew our own vision of who we are and how we can most truly live our baptismal dignity. For example, we can mistake severe depression for loss of faith or the irritability characteristic of the illness for impatience. We see symptoms of our illness as enormous failures in responding to God. The sacrament of Reconciliation is a place to bring all of our chaos into contact with the healing love of the Lord Jesus. How can you do this?

First, if possible, choose one priest with whom you feel comfortable celebrating the sacrament. When you have found a priest you feel you can trust, ask him if you could make an appointment for Reconciliation once a month or so (or arrange your schedule to match the confession schedule of the parish). Second, gradually share with him pertinent information about your diagnosis or what you are going through, providing him a context for what you bring before the Lord in the sacrament. Third, tell the priest what makes you feel guilty. As mentioned, those who suffer with depression or other emotional problems can find it difficult to distinguish between sin and the power of disorderly emotions. Depression can distort our vision of self. In the sacrament of Reconciliation, you can get God's perspective on your life.

It is very helpful to return to the same priest for this sacrament, because he will better understand your particular difficulties and circumstances. I used to go to confession to various priests, but the particular difficulties I experienced as a direct consequence of depression were often misunderstood because they did not know me or my story.

> *"Sometimes even to live is an act of courage."*
> Seneca

I received widely differing advice, some less helpful than others, because the priests had no context in which to understand what I said. When I found a priest whom I could trust to understand my situation, I was able to share my story, my struggles, and my day-to-day attempts to live according to the Gospel. Once I learned from him how to distinguish the effects of depression from sin, I was able to experience the compassion the Lord had for me. My confessor was able to help me discover how God was acting in my life, and, as he helped me to accept my struggle with depression for what it was, I began to feel awed by God's presence and gentle healing.

Frequently, depression follows upon being hurt. Whether someone bears the scars of childhood abuse, or mourns the loss of a loved one, somewhere at the root of their pain is the wondrous possibility of forgiveness: forgiving others, forgiving ourselves, or even forgiving God. The regular celebration of Reconciliation while working through personal issues with a therapist or counselor can bring the gentle healing gift of grace that will gradually bring us to this point of forgiveness, an essential element to acquiring emotional health.

What a relief it is to know that it's not all up to us! We can connect to the Church, to the community of believers, to Jesus' mercy through the sacrament of Reconciliation, the sacrament of healing. We can count on God standing *with* us and *for* us in our journey toward well-being.

We Can Trust the Healing Process

Any healing is miraculous, and even when it is impossible to feel that we believe in anything at all, miraculously God is *still* healing us. Generally healing will be gradual. It is rarely dramatic. Frequently it comes under the simple gesture of one person reaching out to another. In unexpected places, and through unsuspecting people, God comes into our lives. Through one person's illness, God may heal another person who offers to help. One person's journey of healing may be another person's salvation. Or, through a person's depression, God may help the sufferer discover a deeper meaning in life. It is all a mystery. What we do know, however, is that God is laboring within everyone and everything for our salvation. God holds us tightly. He will never let go. Healing is a process. It takes time. But we can trust the process no matter how long it takes. Nothing is ever a detour in our life.

Healing can begin when we admit that we cannot cure ourselves. We need to say "yes" to our powerlessness and stop demanding miracles on *our* terms. When we demand things of God, we keep running away from where we are and, in so doing, we do not allow ourselves to be healed. Our willingness to experience our powerlessness already includes the beginning of surrender to God's action in us. The more we relinquish power over our life, the more we will get in touch with the One who can heal us.

Suggestion for prayer

Here is a summary of the sacrament of Reconciliation if you would like to celebrate this gift of God's mercy:

Prepare. Take some time to prayerfully recall positive moments of light, grace, unexpected goodness, and peace in your life since your last confession. What do these moments say to you? Be concrete, write it down. Then reflect upon what is troubling you about your life. Are there choices, ways of reasoning, behaviors, desires that directly weaken your relationship with God, the Church, others, or yourself? Are there aspects of your life that make you sad, confused, or frustrated that you would like to bring before the Lord? In what ways has God blessed you or have you grown since your last confession?

Make an appointment to celebrate the sacrament. You can phone your parish to speak with a priest, or speak with a priest you know, or go to confession at the time scheduled in your parish.

Know that you are welcome. You and the priest may greet each other. The priest may urge you to have confidence in God. If the priest is your regular confessor, you might want to say anything that you would like him to know.

Confess your sins. Let the priest know your sins. You can take this time to discuss difficulties you are having, for example, "Father, I know I should be much more loving to my children, but with this new medicine I am taking, I barely get any sleep at night. I am so tired. But I want to bring before the Lord my sorrow at not being able to be there more for my children during these weeks, and ask God for the strength to grow in love and patience, as well as in gratitude to my husband who has been extra patient with me." The priest may talk with you about what you have said.

Receive your penance. The priest will recommend a prayer or an action you can do to indicate the sincerity of your sorrow. If it sounds too difficult, let him know.

Pray for forgiveness. The priest will invite you to say a prayer of sorrow aloud. You can pray a traditional prayer of sorrow or speak to God in your own words.

Receive absolution. The priest proclaims the words of absolution and God forgives your sins.

Conclude. The priest may say, "Give thanks to the Lord for he is good." If so, answer, "His mercy endures for ever." Or, he may conclude informally.

As soon as possible after your confession, complete the penance the priest has given you.

⌒๑ ✳ ๑⌒

For one who is depressed

Write down a history of your depression, looking especially for the little "miracles" along the way that show God's presence and care. These might be people who came into your life, experiences you have had, an answer to a prayer, information, or treatment that gave you a new understanding of your illness, reconciliation with a friend or family member, or a felt sense of God's presence when you were walking outside or praying.

For a friend

The sacrament of Reconciliation can also be a privileged space for you as a friend of someone suffering from depression. By sharing the ins and outs, the difficulties and struggles of such a friendship, the sacrament can become a place where real growth in love and self-giving can occur. Share the context of your struggles and limitations (you needn't share names), as well as where you feel you have been self-serving rather than self-giving with your friend. Reconciliation is a graced moment in which you can bring before the Lord your joys and desires, your struggles and weaknesses, a place where God can re-create you little by little as a friend after his own heart.

Basics for Surviving Depression

- Get eight good hours of sleep each night. Don't stay in bed longer or cut your sleep shorter.

- Take a walk between 11:00 A.M. and 2:00 P.M. The bright light has an antidepressant effect. The exercise gives you more energy.

- Abstain from the use of alcohol and street drugs, both of which induce depression and prevent antidepressants from working effectively.

- Eat a well-balanced diet.

- Create a schedule for yourself.

- Take medication as prescribed.

- Avoid the use of products that contain aspartame (for example, Equal or NutraSweet). Studies have shown that these products can increase a person's depression if he or she is already depressed.

- Get a bird or another easy-to-care-for pet. The pet provides company and can also be a conversation starter when talking with friends.

- Choose a friend that you can check in with every day. A depressed person can find it difficult to get out of a rut or a destructive pattern of thinking. Even a phone conversation lasting just a few minutes can be sufficient to help you see a different perspective. A consistent phone call "appointment" can punctuate the "forever" feeling of depression.

- Daily exercise, even as simple as a brisk walk, will give you more energy.

- Keep a journal.

⤳ 4 ⤲

"How Do I Start?"

"The only person who can choose to live your life is you. You must decide for yourself that you want to deal with the pain." *Ruth*

"One Good Friday, I was particularly tried by mental anguish and struggled with these thoughts. I was close to despair. Then, all of a sudden, I heard Jesus say, 'You are sharing in my mental sufferings during the passion.' I felt suddenly at peace and made an act of abandonment to God and again tried to accept my illness." *Linda*

I met Leanne, a colleague at Weston Jesuit School of Theology, on the day of our graduation. She was such a gentle and spiritual person that I would have never guessed the struggles she had been through in the past three years, except for a few hints she let slip here and there in our conversation. She said briefly that her husband had divorced her during her time at Weston, and that the presence of her three teenage children at the graduation Mass and ceremony was very meaningful to her.

> Facing the end of my twenty-two year marriage, raising three teenagers in the face of a loss that has changed their lives forever, dealing with serious physical problems (I had two major surgeries in the same year), and struggling through theology school brought about significant issues of depression for me.

> The high achieving perfectionist part of my personality has somehow always been "held in check" by the other extreme of my personality: the caregiver. I just can't do it "good" enough for myself, and I just can't "give" enough to others. Addressing my new life-struggles involved surrender in order to realize that help was needed for a lady in search of a new identity, someone who was lost in the depths of perfection, caregiving, and loving everyone...except herself.

> One day following my second surgery, I can remember lying on the living room floor, feeling extremely helpless. I was hurting inside and out. My hip was sore from surgery and my heart was sore from isolation and physical immobility. Only the year before, I had run seven miles every day. Now here I was lying down and looking across the room at the crutches I knew I would be depending on for a long time. My mother was there to help me and without her unyielding support, I don't think I would have made it. The presence in the room on that particular day was marked by a very special peace, in spite of the pain. I began to cry. Mom said to me, "It is time that you got some emotional help." She paused for a moment and

added, "You have been in physical pain for nearly a year now, your husband is verbally abusing you, you have three children who love you very much and who are hurting more than you can know. Leanne, you are special, and you can get through this. You can get the help that you really want and that you really need."

I got up and called my primary care physician for the name of some psychotherapists. He gave me a list of names, one of whom was his wife. He told me she was a deeply spiritual person and that I should contact her. I immediately called her, and my journey began.

When I started therapy, I also sought spiritual direction. This involved a weekly commitment to the spiritual exercises of St. Ignatius. The priest who was my spiritual director was extremely helpful in guiding me through a way of praying that encouraged me to *ask* God for hope and healing. You see, I never felt worthy to ask God to rid me of my pain.

My therapist helped me to unravel a journey that had begun with my sister's death when I was just five years old. Carrying the blame for her failure to beat her cancer was something I had never let go of. For many years, I had felt that there had to have been something more I should have done to *save her*. Naturally, I had grown up with the sincere notion that I had to keep everyone I loved from dealing with any pain or suffering. With these roots securely in place, I had much work to do to give myself permission to experience and work through the grief I had stored up within me. Among many other things, I had to free myself from the burden of my sister's death.

I also began to understand that depression develops when people don't have a true sense of who they are and what they are about. There was no such thing as self-identity in my book....

For two years I worked with my therapist and my spiritual director. I felt blessed that both appreciated and respected their role in my healing process. Medically, I remained committed to physical therapy, exercise, and a very mild dose of Prozac. The pain came and went. I stood up and made it through very trying days. I also fell down and crashed many times over, only to get up again, stronger, and more determined to run this race.

I gave myself the gift of a support network of loving friends, my pastor, and my professors. People watched me make my way and reached out to me in many more ways than I could have imagined. Most importantly, I learned to accept their love and their support. In the end, I was able to learn who I am, what it is that I am all about, and that I must love myself more and more and more.

My relationship with God grew deeper and deeper. The intimate presence of God through my difficult days taught me about suffering. I learned to pray in such a way that I gradually realized how close God was to me. I learned to trust, to surrender, to hope, and to love. I learned that I was "on the journey" upward, that I was making my ascent toward God— a God of hope, healing, and love.

If you, like Leanne, have suffered from depression long enough or know someone who has, then you know how seemingly insurmountable are the obstacles to emotional well-being. This chapter is about the first steps you can take.

Educate Yourself

Find out all you can about mood disorders: Go on-line and do research. Read books. Ask questions of your doctor. Take self-tests which you can find on-line or in books. While none of these sources will be completely comprehensive, all knowledge gained empowers you to make decisions that are more informed. You will have to make many choices during your journey to wellness, including choices about treatment options, lifestyle modifications, career assessments, decisions about relationships, living space, and leisure. You may discover that your frustration with a career choice is adding to your depression and a new path may open up to you. If you are a parent, you may also find yourself rethinking your parenting style. A destructive relationship or particularly unhealthy eating habits may contribute to your depression. The more you know about mood disorders and their causes the more you can become a partner in your own treatment.

First Things First

There is no one answer for everyone. However, the first step toward surviving depression is the same for everyone. Have a complete physical examination with a physician you trust. Make follow-up appointments for any other specialists to whom you are referred. Ask that copies of all your medical records from follow-up appointments be referred to the physician who did the initial physical examination. If you are not getting answers, pursue appointments with doctors who are specifically trained in psychological or neurological issues.

Conflicting diagnoses for depression or mood disorders are common. When Tye was diagnosed by a psychiatrist as having a slight mood disorder, he began taking the prescribed medication. Though he went ahead with the medication for several months while meeting with his psychiatrist weekly, something just didn't seem right to him. He didn't find his sessions helpful and was unsatisfied with the medication he was taking, but the doctor was unwilling to explore other possibilities. After almost a year, Tye decided to get another opinion. The new doctor was able to pinpoint the type of depression he was suffering from and prescribed a different medication. Within weeks, Tye began to feel good again.

Learning all you can about mood disorders and insisting that you get the appropriate testing is essential for correct treatment. If cost is a problem, other payment options are available. Consult a hospital in your area or ask your doctor for information.

Commit Yourself to the Process

As a person is diagnosed and possible causes ruled out, two things can happen. First, a person may start to feel better quickly and, as a result, cut short the continued investigation of possibilities that such disorders generally require. I have seen this happen so often. I know someone whose general practitioner prescribed a medication for depression, and encouraged him to see a psychologist. Since he felt so good immediately after beginning his medication, he never made an appointment with a psychologist, but continued taking the medication. Several years later, friends who noted his mood swings again encouraged him to see a psychologist. After appropriate testing, it became evident that while he felt "wonderful," the prescribed medication was contributing to his increasing emotional instability. He was placed on a small dosage of another medication and began therapy to resolve underlying issues.

> *"There is a time for everything: a time to weep and a time to laugh, a time to mourn and a time to dance."*
> Ecclesiastes 3:4

Second, some people, after giving their doctor one—and only one—chance to "make them feel better," decide to switch doctors without bringing their history with them. Geri had been to four or five different doctors before I met her. If she decided that she didn't trust what one doctor was telling her, she went on to another. Each of the successive doctors did not know her history, and, therefore, none of them were able to get to the source of her problems. After you find a doctor you are comfortable with, give him or her a chance to help you. It will take many informed attempts and tests to narrow down what exactly is at the root of the problems you are experiencing. Keep your own record of appointments, tests you have had, doctors' recommendations, medications you have been prescribed, any reactions, etc. Although when you see a new doctor you should insist that your medical records be sent to him or her, documenting your medical situation yourself will be very valuable.

The journey to wellness may take years. After a correct diagnosis, the search for the right medication begins. There are many drugs on the market. Be sure to ask about possible side effects. Once you begin medication, it is important to share with your doctor any reactions or difficulties you experience. Usually, you will begin to have an indication of how the medication is helping with your mood disorder after two or three weeks. Don't be embarrassed to keep informing your doctor how you feel. In the end, you should be feeling "good." Don't be satisfied with less. The doctor may need to change the dosage or prescription, add another medication, or recommend therapy, behavioral or lifestyle changes, or diet modification. Many aspects of your treatment will need to be balanced to attain emotional well-being. Be patient and work with your doctor. Your treatment will be as unique as you are.

Don't Leave It All to Medication

Medication is not always the whole answer. Twenty-year-old Ruth, presently studying social work at a large Catholic university, was prescribed appropriate medication for her depression and began counseling. As time went on, Ruth's symptoms grew less severe and continued decreasing. Now, five years after having begun treatment, Ruth no longer needs medication. Her program for wholeness included some time on medication, regular counseling, lifestyle modification, and behavior challenges, along with daily participation in the Eucharistic celebration. Although medication may be a large part of your treatment, there are many issues related to your depression that can't be "medicated" away. After my doctor had tried combinations of several medications, he suggested therapy, for at least a short period, so that he could determine what other issues were involved in my depression. Through therapy, I was able to identify some of these issues and work to resolve them, and consequently I was able to minimize the medication I needed.

In looking for a therapist, try to find someone who has extensive experience and knowledge of your type of illness. If you are seriously depressed or bipolar, make sure that the therapist has a backup when on vacation or otherwise unavailable. In your first interviews, see if the therapist communicates an attitude of caring and interest. You can find good therapists often through the recommendation of other people, through mental health organizations, or through your psychiatrist. Your parish office might also be able to give you a recommendation of a Catholic therapist in your area.

It takes enormous courage to commit to therapy. When you give yourself fully to the process and you begin to explore your issues, it can seem that things get worse before they get better. It's important to tell your therapist how you think things are going. If you think that things are going well, say so, but also be frank if you think your therapist is making connections or drawing conclusions that do not make sense to you. If you think you and your therapist aren't working well together, let him or her know. The key is to explore these issues with the therapist, and not make snap decisions on your own. *You* have to claim responsibility for your journey to well-being, but work *with* your therapist.

Consider Joining a Support Group

The people who best understand depression or bipolar mood swings are people who have been or are depressed or bipolar themselves. It can be healing to be with people who have similar problems. In a support group, you don't need to hide your problems. People there understand. Support groups can also be a good source of information on mood disorders and tips on handling problems associated with mood swings.

To locate support groups in your area, call your local mental health help line or contact local mental health facilities. Not all support groups are the same. If one doesn't meet your needs, you might try exploring another. Make sure you join a support group that is constructive for you.

The Church as Spiritual Hospital

The journey to emotional health and wholeness is not restricted entirely to the sphere of psychology. To this day Eastern Orthodox spirituality has preserved its understanding of the human person, which permeated the writings of the desert fathers and mothers, writers, and theologians of the East. Writers such as St.

Gregory of Nyssa (335–395), St. Gregory Palamas (1296–1359), and St. John of Sinai (c. 579–649), among others, believed that illnesses of the human psyche and heart are best addressed by theology. St. John of Sinai, for instance, saw the journey to wholeness as a journey from isolated individuality toward a relationship with God, with the community, with oneself, and with all of creation. Because the "cure" for someone suffering from depression or other illnesses is a journey from an inward love to a love that reaches out to God and others, these Christians believed that this process needs to take place in a spiritual climate. They saw the Church as a "spiritual hospital."

"There is another way, if you have the courage. [This] way is unknown, and so requires faith— the kind of faith which issues from despair.
...But the way leads toward possession of what you have sought for in the wrong place."
T. S. Eliot

Today we live in a society that fosters individualism, a society in which people are separated from each other and the possibility of community and communion. Even many parish communities have lost much of their communal nature, and we can find ourselves slipping in and out of the Eucharistic liturgy without knowing anyone else in the church, without a greeting or even a glance. Because God created us in the image and likeness of God, however, he created us for relationship. We were created to have and to maintain a relationship with

God, with others, and with the whole of creation. In fact, Adam and Eve lived this way until they lost their orientation toward God by grasping for the illusory promise of autonomy, of becoming like God. In this sense, health *is* real and true relationship. Illness is the interruption of that relationship, the essential dialogue with God, with one's brothers and sisters, with oneself, and with creation. The Church is the "hospital" where we can rediscover the essential communion that our first parents lost, for the center of the Christian community is God, and health flourishes when we become truly what God has meant the human person to be.

What Lies within Us

God became human in Christ to show us what it really means to be human, that is, to share in God's life. The one who denies his or her relationship with God is like a story that is half-finished, or a building that has been abandoned before completion. Each person "has a capacity to let loose in him or herself the Risen Christ." When the Risen Christ is "let loose" in us, God's image is renewed and restored, we are once more in communion with God through the Holy Spirit, and we participate in the kingdom of God, and by grace become what God is by nature. Maximus the Confessor (580–649) wrote, "Man by the grace of God can become that which God is." The Fathers of the Church called this transfiguration and transformation *theosis*. We are given the power to get up and walk out of a crippled past into a life of new meaning, joined to others in community, in peace with God, with ourselves, and with all of creation.

What does this say to those suffering from depression? In the words of Ralph Waldo Emerson, "What lies behind us, and what lies before us, are small matters compared to what lies within us." To those struggling with emotional and psychological pain *theosis* says that they have the capacity through the power of God to transcend and overcome any and every difficulty. *Theosis* tells us that we are sons and daughters of God, we share in God's glory, we partake of God's nature, we are destined to inherit God's eternal kingdom. Scripture tells us that we will "inherit" the kingdom. Inheritance implies ownership. We won't just slip in the back door—the kingdom will *belong* to us as much as it belongs to our "co-heir," Jesus Christ. In this spiritual hospital that is the community of believers, we learn that in all the sorrows and pain of depression, we are "more than conquerors through God who has loved us" (cf. Rm 8:37).

Russian religious philosopher, Vladimir Soloviev, wrote:

> If you wish to be upraised unto God; if you wish to be so united with God that God is all in you; if you despair because, eager to share in the divine nature, you have only a glimpse of it, then take assurance. The Father, the Son, and the Holy Spirit are calling you, indeed, to ascend unto them. They are ready to come down toward you and in you, in order to live as the habitual guests of your soul. They promise to your whole being, in exchange for what is good in it, a transformation, at first mysterious and invisible,

but soon resplendent and glorious, a union and assimilation that will divinize you.[1]

At the root of our "cure" is a personal act of faith in the love of God. "There is no greater love," said St. Angela of Foligno, "than for God to become man to make me god." No matter how hard the struggle is, we can hang in there with the spirit of St. Paul who stated his faith in these words, "I consider that the sufferings of this present time are not worth comparing with the glory about to be revealed in us" (Rm 8:18).

––––––––––

Suggestion for prayer

Depression brings with it darkness and chaos. But God is present within as Light, Peace, and Love. God is stronger than all the pain. The darkness is passing, the Light is forever. The darkness comes only from wounds for which we ourselves are often not responsible. The Light defines us as God's sons and daughters. Try praying the following:

You, Lord, are present in me as Light. Nothing can take the Light from me. You have chosen me to be your child. You hold me tight. Nothing can take me from you. The darkness and chaos will come and go as I am healed. But you, O Lord, will remain, because I am forever yours.

Write this prayer out for yourself and keep it with you so that you can pray it often.

––––––––––

1. Anthony M. Coniaris, "Achieving Your Potential in Christ: Theosis." August 21, 2003, www.geocities.com/verseoftheday/theosis3.htm.

ᥰᨘ ✻ ᥰᨘ

For one who is depressed

Write in a small notebook the names of the doctors and/or therapists you have seen, tests you remember having had, medications you have taken (as well as any major reactions or side effects that you remember), and your present medications and dosage. Keep the notebook in a place where you will remember it. If you haven't had a complete medical check-up in a while, or you have changed doctors or therapists frequently and your present doctor doesn't have a complete history, bring this to her or his attention.

Do you have an acquaintance in your parish or someone you know who goes to the same Mass as you? A parish can be a source of stability and support, even if it is only through one or two people that you meet each Sunday at Mass. If you don't have any contacts in your parish, start by greeting others before and after the Sunday liturgy, or at other parish functions you may attend.

For a friend

Has your friend taken the first necessary steps toward well-being listed in this chapter? If not, share this information with him or her.

Internet Resources for Support

Depression and Bipolar Support Alliance
www.dbsalliance.org

National Alliance for the Mentally Ill
www.nami.org

Depressed Anonymous (a twelve step program)
www.depressedanon.com

National Foundation for Depressive Illnesses
www.depression.org

Anxiety Disorders Association of America
www.adaa.org

Center for Mental Health Services
www.mentalhealth.org

Federation of Families for Children's Mental
Health www.ffcmh.org

_⚬ 5 ⚬_

"I Just Want to Feel Better"

"I ask God every day to take this away and make me happy again. I don't think God hears me. Maybe God is sick of me asking." _Gerard_

———————

"I do a lot of my recovery work in prayer. I talk to God about what I feel now, and about the trauma I experienced in the past. God listens to me. He gives me the courage and strength I need to get through the times I feel more depressed." _Fr. Joseph_

If you want to be happy again then you have to start doing something yourself. I had to learn over and over again that if I waited around for _my_ kind of miracle, I would have to wait a long time. Not that I don't believe in miracles. I do. I have simply come to realize, however, that God's idea of the miraculous is sometimes an ongoing process of a deeper connection with God. So I've learned not to shortchange myself by insisting on miracles *my* way. If I could, I would rid myself of Temporal Lobe Epilepsy and have a perfectly stable personality. *Just think of all the things I could do if I were free from these mood swings,* I say to myself. But if I consume my energy wishing for something beyond my control and use it as a test of whether God has or hasn't heard my prayers, I set myself up for disappointment. Instead of "answering my prayers" exactly as I want, God looks into my heart and responds to the deeper desires that he sees there, desires God himself has put within me. Perhaps he sees that I am asking for a penny when he wants to give me a million dollars. When I would be content to do something that makes me feel reasonably good about myself, God knows that I actually desire so much more. And so he takes the liberty to work the miracles I don't even know to ask for.

Miracles Do Happen

Though we can't create them or command miracles, miracles do happen—gradually. Often we discover them only when we look back over our lives. We can see the gentle hand of God, the merciful caress of divine love threaded through the experiences of each day. We often see how God's power was hidden even in the efforts we made to help ourselves.

John, a college professor for thirty-two years, is married and the father of five. A few years ago, he went through a six-month period of deep depression. "They were the worst six months of my life," he says. "I was ashamed and confused. I still keep it a secret. Because

I've been in therapy ever since that time, full-blown depression has never returned." John believes that he had suffered from depression all of his life and never knew it.

Two years after he began therapy, John went to Medjugorje on a pilgrimage to pray for healing. "I thought I would come back healed. When I returned home, my doctor suggested we try another medication, which made all the difference. It took care of my insomnia, irritability, and self-pity. I've been on this medication ever since. My healing came, but in a form I didn't expect."

John believes he has been a better servant to his students because of his familiarity with depression. He has been able to help young people suffering from depression get the help they need, and he has been able to support their families. John has taught music, theater, German, and courses in education. The creativity that often comes with depression—and which allows John to express himself in so many different areas—has been a gift to him in his career. "A lot of depressed people achieve great things. I believe it is the illness of creative people. Many musicians, artists, and poets have suffered from depression. Actually, if the Lord had healed me at Medjugorje, it might have ruined other things."

Prayer keeps John from sinking too low. "Sometimes I can't pray. I just say, 'Jesus.' Somehow I know my prayers are heard." Prayer is also a bond between John and his wife. "My wife has been a huge support to me. We say simple prayers together every evening. In the morning, we pray the morning offering. Praying together relieves a lot of tension for my wife because it isn't easy living with someone who is mentally ill."

The New Gifts Discovered in Depression

For the person suffering from depression, miracles come in many shapes and sizes. There is a legend of a bird in a forest full of animal friends. The bird was known for her swift flight, and thus she was called *She who flies swiftly*. The magnificent coloring of her wings flashed in the sunlight as she soared in and out of the trees of the forest. One day *She who flies swiftly* broke a wing. She fell to the forest floor, and dragged herself near a tree for safety. After a little while, the Lord of the forest found *She who flies swiftly*. He gently picked up the frightened bird and passed his hands over her broken wing before putting her down. The other birds were delighted. They thought, certainly *She who flies swiftly* would be darting about through the forest once more. But *She who flies swiftly* still wasn't able to fly. Instead, she stayed beneath a tree, lifting up her sad voice to the sky. The mournful notes continued through the days and nights, becoming always stronger and stronger. The forest had never heard the beauty of her song before. In the night hours, the other forest animals would quiet down and listen to her music, which grew more and more beautiful. *She who flies swiftly* had learned to sing out of the depths of her sorrow and her loss, and her music captivated the hearts of all who heard it. *She who flies swiftly* never flew again, but the healing touch of the Lord of the forest had given her the miracle of song and a new direction in life.

Those with the courage to walk *all* the way through the journey of depression discover the new gifts they are given. That is why John could remark, "Looking back on my life I wouldn't want to change anything."

Starting with the Basics

Getting out of bed

The little miracles that God brings about in our life include such basic things as the strength to get out of bed in the morning. Those suffering from depression know how hard this can be when any day, every day, *all* day is one black hole of the overwhelming effort just to live. They just want the struggle with depression to end. They don't want to wake up to the same thing day after day.

But healing starts in small ways. With the help of a therapist or friend, choose an appropriate time for rising. Make an agreement that this is the start of your day. Set the alarm clock next to you, along with a reminder that this is your agreement. Sometimes being responsible to someone you respect or who knows you is a helpful motivation. From the small things done daily you can build up to new habits that can facilitate your journey to healing.

Diet

A sense of well-being is often connected to the care we take of our bodies. What we eat affects how we feel. Fruits and vegetables have a better effect on moods than do junk foods high in fat, sugar, and salt. Sugar is the number one culprit for mood altering substances. It can cause mood elevation, hyperactivity, fatigue, mood instability, depression, exaggerated moods, headaches, irritability, and distorted and exaggerated anxiety. Avoiding foods high in sugar can be the first step toward a diet that assists your growth to wholeness.

Another culprit is caffeine. For many, simply being more conscious of caffeine intake is a good start to lessening the intensity of mood swings. Because many depend on that first cup of coffee in the morning, or coffee breaks throughout the day, it may be difficult to monitor caffeine intake. It is helpful to find another beverage you enjoy as much (other than tea, cola, or hot chocolate which are also high in caffeine) in order to gradually reduce the amount of caffeinated beverages consumed each day.

"Keep your face to the sunshine and you cannot see your shadow."
Helen Keller

Some people have also found dairy products to be a contributing factor to their mood swings, as well as wheat products, eggs, meat, and tomatoes.

You may be asking yourself if there is anything left to eat that will promote mood stability. If you speak with your doctor and a nutritionist, they can help you make a plan for a healthy diet that will promote your well-being. Your doctor will also be able to inform you if weight gain/loss is a side effect of the medication you are taking. Together you can discuss diet modification and exercise to deal with any weight gain or loss.

Exercise

The value of exercise for physical and mental well-being is constantly before our eyes. It is almost impossible to flip through a magazine without encountering at least one ad for exercise equipment, gyms, or exercise classes. Even ads for medication use pictures of people cycling or walking to "advertise" a healthy lifestyle. We are a health-conscious generation, at least "in theory."

Maybe you've looked at such ads and turned the page. If you are depressed, just seeing the trim, perfect bodies of the models in these ads can make you feel even worse about your own appearance. It seems much less threatening to stay at home and say you'll find a way to exercise on your own. *After all,* you tell yourself, *it just takes going for a walk....* But somehow, that walk never happens. Or maybe it happens once. Good exercise habits may be difficult to start, especially if weight gain is a side effect of your medication. Nevertheless, exercise will make you feel better. The hardest step is actually beginning. Here are some ideas to help get you started:

- Choose a form of exercise you can enjoy, perhaps swimming, dancing, or yoga.

- If you choose to walk, find an exercise tape or lively, upbeat music to walk with.

- Plan to walk through a park a few times a week with a fellow employee or friend.

- Offer to help someone who gardens and commit yourself to once or twice a week.

- Join an exercise program or a gym if a membership will help you commit to exercise.

Light

Just being outdoors for a half hour each day is the most inexpensive way to avail yourself of the powerful effects of light on your mood. When I go for a long walk after having worked indoors for several days, I quickly feel my spirits lifting. Today more and more research is being done regarding the power of light for elevating mood.

The next best thing to soaking in light from the sun is to use full-spectrum lighting where you live and work. Full-spectrum lighting contains the same rainbow colors and the same amount of near ultraviolet light as sunlight. You can purchase full-spectrum lighting (Vita-Lit is one trade name) at a hardware store.

Some people seem to need more sunlight than others. Certain seasons of the year with shorter and darker days seem to bring down some people's moods and increase their depression. People who experience depression during these darker seasons may have Seasonal Affective Disorder (SAD). Exposing yourself to sunlight or full-spectrum light even for just these times of the year may be an unexpected key to lifting your spirits.

The miracle of coming out of a depression or learning to live graciously with a persistent mood disorder takes a combination of physical, psychological, and spiritual insight.

Dream

Despite the inner pain, depression does have its "advantages" and there are people who would rather stay depressed in order make use of them. My depression and the problems caused by my stroke were serious enough to begin with, but they became a self-ful-filling prophecy over the years. My self-confidence had been so destroyed that the "safety-net" of being "sick" was preferable to the unknown adventure of taking on new responsibility and launching out into the unknown. If I spoke my mind, if I tried to motivate people, if I carried through on a project despite others' comments, I would have to leave the comfort zone of depression behind. I would no longer have a ready excuse for failure. I wouldn't have a cocoon to return to in order to nurse my wounds. I would expose myself to the evaluation of others instead of remaining safely out of reach where I could judge them. As you begin to heal, it can happen that a powerful struggle occurs between the "depressed" you and the you that desires to move on.

When we have the possibility of stepping into the unknown, of risking failure, of beginning to live without "depression" written across our foreheads, we can unconsciously sabotage ourselves so that we remain in the safety net of being able to blame our failure on depression. After all, people probably don't expect much from us out of kindness and compassion for our situation. Acting with responsibility in a new venture where our success or failure is determined solely by how well we handle ourselves can be very frightening. To accept the challenge of doing what we haven't done for months or years will draw attention. What if we fail? If we fail, we have simply proven that we are as human as the next person is. However, there are some tools, which can make the first steps less ominous.

First, get past mental blocks. Begin listing the names of the people in your life who have believed in you. Who have been good role models in your life? What have you appreciated most about them? Before you became depressed, what was the one thing that ruined your chance of being successful at something you really wanted? What negative lesson did you learn? Is this lesson really true? Are you still letting it rule your life? What about yourself now makes you the most proud?

"Miracles are the ordinary revealed in their simple splendor."
Rabbi Pirke Avot

What do you think God sees when he looks at you? List the skills for which you are most grateful. Name three things you'd really like to do. If you could be anything, what three things would you be? If you had to ask God for the one thing most important to you, what would it be? What makes you most excited?

Next, take new steps—one at a time. Perhaps you feel something stirring inside: *I would like to try out for a new position. I wonder if I could teach that class. I would love to work on that project. I would be so happy if I could bring a sense of beauty to our home again.* After you settle on a goal, list for yourself the steps you *think* you should follow to achieve it. Then rip up the list and begin to enumerate things you *wish* you could do in order to achieve your goal. What you *wish* you could do will probably be more outlandish than what you *think* you can do, but that's okay, here the sky is the limit. Then, finally, list what you really feel like doing. What do you really see yourself doing? Find a place of prayer: a church, your room, a favorite place outdoors or in a park. One by one, present to God what you have written down: your dreams, your feelings, seemingly farfetched impossibilities... Pay attention to your initial reaction to these ideas as you present them to God. Do you feel light, happy, excited, confident, and at peace? Or are there some ideas that leave you feeling negative, fearful, closed in on yourself, cut off from God or others? Over several weeks, bring these ideas to prayer, asking God to help you see God's dream for you rooted in your heart. As you begin to cross out ideas that leave you with a dead feeling, begin to concentrate your attention on the ideas that leave you with a feeling of life and hope. Ask God to show you how you can best achieve your goal in a way that is good for yourself, that serves others, and that pleases God. When you and God have decided on a direction, ask God to bless it. As you begin taking steps toward your goal, pay attention to what you feel within your heart. You can repeat steps of this process as often as needed, asking God for direction and strength.

It is strange but true that we "get" something out of depression, even as it drains us of life. By unmasking our attempts of self-sabotage we can walk into a future of hope, God's dream for us, written in the depths of our hearts.

Suggestion for prayer

The sign of the cross is a prayer of blessing made by tracing with our right hand the figure of the cross on our forehead, our breast, our shoulders, and saying, "In the name of the Father, and of the Son, and of the Holy Spirit. Amen." The sign of the cross symbolizes God blessing us, God embracing us with blessings. We recall the death of Jesus on the cross, a death that was an outpouring of love for us. The sign of the cross is a reminder of this forever love, a love that, as we sign ourselves with the cross, abides in us forever. Make the sign of the cross often. As you make this simple gesture, let it remind you that you are blessed in mind and heart and all your being. Through this prayer, which you can pray any time in the day or night, let God bring calm, and peace, and comfort to you. "Come to me," God says through this prayer. "Do not be afraid. Before you take one step, I reach out to embrace you and bless you."

⋙

For one who is depressed

When a person is depressed it is difficult to begin cultivating healthy habits. Choose two or three concrete suggestions from this chapter that you can begin doing even in a small way.

For a friend

Express to your friend that you know God has a dream for him or her and that it will be clear in time. Support your friend through any changes he or she has decided to make.

Strategies for Raising Your Self-Esteem:

- Celebrate your accomplishments.

- Be content with less than perfection.

- Realize that you haven't been beat; you're working through your problems.

- Accept that it may take longer to accomplish your goals.

- Take things in stride.

- Make sure that you talk with people who support you.

- Think of yourself as a good and positive person.

- Believe in yourself as a child of God.

- Pray to the Trinity within you.

- Believe others who affirm your worth.

- Know that mental illness is no cause for shame.

- Determine to get more out of life.

- Realize that those who treat you poorly are saying more about themselves than about you.

- Live one day at a time.

- Do work that you feel good doing.

- Pursue hobbies and crafts.

- Use creative expression (draw, paint, write, dance, etc.).

- Take small risks in a safe place.

- Be around people you like and who like you.

- Write down all the things that are good about yourself.

- Educate others around you about mood disorders and self-esteem issues.

__∽ 6 ∾__

"I Can't Stop Crying"

"The hardest thing I ask of myself is 'Why me?'" *Juan*

"God has a dream for me and somehow, somewhere, this is all part of that dream. I learned to stop fighting and listen instead to God's voice calling me. In hindsight this experience of depression has lead me to be able to slowly become the 'compassion of Christ' for others." *Ralph*

Once a man received a letter from a business executive which stated he wanted to hand over to him a large sum of money. The gentleman didn't say where the money had come from or upon what conditions the money would be given. He only said to expect him within a year.

Now the surprised recipient of this good news took a long look around his house and thought about his job and friends. Obviously, he would have to make some changes before the money-bearing guest arrived. His front lawn would need a face-lift, the interior of his

> *"Christ has turned all our sunsets into dawns."*
> St. Clement of Alexandria

house a fresh coat of paint, and new entertainment equipment purchased somehow. He then began to consider that neither his friends nor his position at the company he worked for would make a favorable impression. Perhaps he had better begin moving in better circles and putting in more hours at his job.

He made a list of what he needed to do before his guest would arrive. He began working on improving his yard, home, and self, while running up bills on his credit card and promising payment for services. He worked extra hours with the hope of gaining a promotion, and for six months barely had time to catch a few hours of sleep before he was up and running again.

Then the long-awaited writer of the letter came to town on a business trip. In between appointments, he called at the man's house several times, but only met the painter or landscaper, who were never sure exactly when the owner of the house would be back. One day, the business executive drove up just as the owner of the house was leaving without so much as a backward glance. So the business executive left a note that read, *May I meet with you? A friend.* And he left a phone number. When the owner returned home, he found the note, but crumpled it up in his hand and tossed it into the garbage. *I don't have time for this,* he thought.

The next morning he opened his front door and in his hurry almost ran over his would-be benefactor. "My friend," the well-dressed gentleman said gently, "I was hoping to speak with you."

"I don't know you," replied the owner walking past hurriedly.

"I know you don't, but may I come over to see you one evening?"

"Look, I'm really very busy; I haven't a free evening for the next two weeks. And I really have to run now."

"As you wish," the gentleman said. "But I really would like to meet with you before I leave town."

"Well, leave your number and I'll see about it."

The executive did as he was asked and went away. At the end of three weeks, his business completed, he reluctantly left town. Upon arriving home he sent a letter to the owner of the house explaining how he had tried to deliver the money, but couldn't since the man seemed to have no time.

When the man received the letter and realized his mistake, he wrote back quickly, "I was busy preparing for your arrival. I wanted to fix things up to be able to welcome you in the way you deserve."

One week later, an envelope appeared in the mailbox. Trembling, he opened the envelope to find three handwritten lines on a single sheet of paper. "You didn't need to do anything for me. I knew all about you. The money was my *gift* to you."

God is the Friend who wants to meet you with a gift. God doesn't need to see in you a perfectly balanced personality before considering you worthy of his gifts. God knows you just as you are, with your history, your fears, your needs and tears that perhaps never seem to stop falling. God loves you just as you are. God is the one who loves you most, with your garbage, limitations, and problems, as well as the beauty that you may not be able to see at this time. Nothing in your life could make you any less beautiful in God's eyes. You do not want to make the mistake of thinking you need to impress God. God is walking toward you always, arms outstretched, able to help you find meaning in everything. What is most needed is that you allow God to impress *you*. Let God impress you with his love. Even if you feel nothing when you read about God's love for you, keep believing. One day you will no longer need to believe, because you will know. I have experienced this myself, and I have seen it in others.

Is Your God Good?

God's love can remain something very abstract. If God's love is to *be real,* people need to build a bridge for themselves between the experience of God's love and the personal experience of being loved by another person. Building on the positive images of actually being loved by someone enables you to experience tangibly God's love for you and to involve your whole person in that experience. Believe that God is at least as loving toward you as some other person who has acknowledged, accepted, or affirmed you. If God isn't as loving as the best people you know, then you do not yet know God. Through Scripture, God reveals the characteristics of his immense love.

God reveals himself as "tender, compassionate, and constant."

The LORD passed before him, and proclaimed, "The LORD, the LORD, a God merciful and gracious, slow to anger, and abounding in steadfast love and faithfulness, keeping steadfast love for the thousandth generation" (Ex 34:6–7).

God's love is expressed as a safe love. God is one on whom we can depend.

When Israel was a child, I loved him, and out of Egypt I called my son. The more I called them, the more they went from me; they kept sacrificing to the Baals, and offering incense to idols. Yet it was I who taught Ephraim to walk, I took them up in my arms; but they did not know that I healed them. I led them with cords of human kindness, with bands of love. I was to them like those who lift infants to their cheeks. I bent down to them and fed them (Hos 11:1–4).

God acknowledges our essential dignity, a dignity that psychological problems cannot touch or diminish.

But now thus says the LORD, he who created you, O Jacob, he who formed you, O Israel: Do not fear, for I have redeemed you; I have called you by name, you are mine. When you pass through the waters, I will be with you; and through the rivers, they shall not overwhelm you; when you walk through fire you shall not be burned, and the flame shall not consume you. For I am the LORD your God, the Holy One of Israel, your Savior. I give Egypt as your ransom, Ethiopia and Seba in exchange for you. Because you are precious in my sight, and honored, and I love you, I give people in return for you, nations in exchange for your life. Do not fear, for I am with you; I will bring your offspring from the east, and from the west I will gather you (Is 43:1–5; Jer 31:31–34).

God appreciates us. He finds his delight in those whom he has created.

The nations shall see your vindication, and all the kings your glory; and you shall be called by a new name that the mouth of the LORD will give. You shall be a crown of beauty in the hand of the LORD, and a royal diadem in the hand of your God. You shall no more be termed Forsaken, and your land shall no more be termed Desolate; but you shall be called My Delight Is in Her, and your land Married; for the LORD delights in you, and your land shall be married. For as a young man marries a young woman, so shall your builder marry you, and as the bridegroom rejoices over the bride, so shall your God rejoice over you (Is 62:2–5).

God is concerned for our welfare.

For surely I know the plans I have for you, says the LORD, plans for your welfare and not for harm, to give you a future with hope (Jer 29:11).

Stake Your Life on God's Love

St. Edith Stein, also known as St. Teresa Benedicta of the Cross, was born into a Jewish family on October 12, 1891. A philosopher who became a Catholic on January 1, 1922, Edith entered a cloistered Carmelite convent and died at Auschwitz.

A brilliant student, Edith graduated with the high-
est honors in 1916, and the well-known philosopher
and phenomenologist, Edmond Husserl, chose her to
be his research and teaching
assistant. Her joy at her own *"There is strong*
success, however, was marred. *shadow where*
All around her there raged *there is much*
World War I, with its hundreds *light."*
of thousands of casualties, caus-
Johann Wolfgang
ing Edith unspeakable suffer- von Goethe
ing. Among the war's victims
was a dear friend, Adolf Reinach, who had first intro-
duced her to Husserl. Though Edith traveled to be with
and console Reinach's widow, she found herself con-
soled by his widow instead.

Edith continued to study, translate, teach, and lec-
ture until 1933, when Hitler's regime and laws stripped
non-Aryans of all their rights and dismissed them from
all professional employment. On April 19, 1933, Edith's
work as a lecturer at the Catholic Pedagogical Institute
of Münster was terminated. She could not ignore the
gathering storm clouds and the hopelessness of her
countrymen, as well as her own sense of foreboding. "I
gradually worked myself into real despair.... I could no
longer cross the street without wishing that a car would
run over me...and I would not come out alive."[2]

During a Eucharistic holy hour at the Carmel of
Cologne, shortly before she joined the community,

---

2. Maria Amata Neyer, OCD, *Edith Stein: Her Life in Photos and Documents,* trans. Waltruat Stein (Washington, D.C.: ICS Publications, 1998) p. 22.

Edith prayed, conscious of the shadow that hung over her beloved Germany. As she continued to pray for her people, she realized

> [I]t was his cross that was being laid on the Jewish people. Most of them did not understand it; but those who did understand must accept it willingly in the name of all. I wanted to do that, let him only show me how. When the service was over, I had an interior conviction that I had been heard. But in what the bearing of the cross was to consist, I did not yet know.[3]

When Edith entered the Carmel of Cologne and later received her new name, Sr. Teresa Benedicta of the Cross, she alluded to this night of prayer:

> I must tell you that I already brought my religious name with me into the house as a postulant. I received it exactly as I requested it. By the cross I understood the destiny of God's people which, even at that time, began to announce itself. I thought that those who recognized it as the cross of Christ had to take it upon themselves in the name of all. Certainly, today I know more of what it means to be wedded to the Lord in the sign of the cross. Of course, one can never apprehend it, for it is a mystery.[4]

Edith Stein's last philosophical work, completed in the monastery for the fourth centenary of the birth of John of the Cross, is entitled, *The Science of the Cross*. After she and her sister, Rosa Stein, were arrested by the SS on August 2, 1942, her superior found the com-

---

3. See Cecily Hastings and Donald Nicholl, trans., *Sister Teresia de Spiritu Sancto [Posselt], Edith Stein* (New York: Sheed and Ward, 1952), p. 118.

4. Edith Stein, *The Science of the Cross*, (Washington, D.C.: Institute of Carmelite Studies, 2003), p. xix.

pleted manuscript lying open, signifying she had worked on it that very day.

Some time later the prioress of the monastery received a letter from Sr. Benedicta dated August 5, 1942, which read, "I am happy about everything. One can gain a science of the cross only if one feels the weight of the cross pressing down with all its force."[5]

On the evening of August 7, 1942, the Stein sisters boarded a train destined for Auschwitz. Together with other women and children, they died in a gas chamber at Auschwitz on August 9, their bodies thrown into a ditch.

Edith Stein left these words, "I believe in God. I believe that the nature of God is love, I believe that man exists in love, is upheld by God, is saved by God."[6] Edith Stein says to those who are depressed: *Stake your life on God's love. Believe in the mystery of the cross.* Even if you are angry with God, believing God has "given you" this illness or these problems, still stake your life on God. Stake your life on the waters of Baptism that still wash your soul. Stake your life on your true dignity as a son or daughter of God. Stake your life on the only One who can keep you safe. Become a silent prophet, pointing to the search for God—the only search that will bring authentic peace.

---

5. Gino Concetti, "Edith Stein," *L'Osservatore Romano,* April 27, 1987, pp. 3–4.

6. Ibid.

Suggestion for prayer

Obtain some holy water from your church to keep in your home. Blessed water reminds us of cleansing and healing. Water is used to clean and to heal. The Church encourages Catholics to bless themselves with holy water when they are in danger from storms, sickness, tragedy, or other calamity. Holy water can be stored in a clean jar or you can purchase a small holy water font that you can hang up in your room. In my family, we always had holy water in each of our rooms as we were growing up. Blessing ourselves with holy water was the first thing we did in the morning and the last thing we did at night. You can pray a short prayer as you bless yourself with holy water, such as, "By this holy water and by your Precious Blood, bring me peace of mind and heart, O Lord."

✦

For one who is depressed

Keep a small notebook by your bed. Each evening write down the names of one or two people who have shown you a glimpse of God's care and concern for you.

For a friend

In a moment of prayer, look over the past few times you have been with your friend who is suffering from depression. Are you happy with the way you have shown care and concern for him or her? Is there something you would like to change? Talk to Jesus about it.

Types of Depression

Depressive disorders come in different forms. There are several diagnoses for depression, mostly determined by the intensity and duration of the symptoms, and the specific cause of the symptoms, if that is known. Depression is a treatable illness. The unique form that it takes in each person means that the treatment will be highly tailored to each individual.

Major or clinical depression

Major depression, also known as clinical depression, is the most serious type of depression, characterized by a combination of severe symptoms that interfere with one's ability to work, sleep, eat, and enjoy once pleasurable activities. Disabling episodes of depression can occur once, twice, or several times in one's life.

Dysthymia

Dysthymia results from long-term chronic symptoms that do not disable a person but keep them from ever feeling good. It is a form of depression that can be far less severe than major depression, although crippling in its own way. This tendency to a depressed mood can result from childhood traumas, difficult life transitions, personal losses, unresolved problems, and chronic stress. Dysthymic disorder is characterized by a steady presence of symptoms (i.e., depressed mood all day for at least two years, difficulties in sleeping, low self-esteem, difficulty concentrating, persistent headaches, etc.), and because it is not as severely incapacitating as clinical depression, it is often left undiagnosed or dismissed but is also treatable.

Manic depression

Less common than major depression, manic-depressive illness maintains a high profile because of the many creative artists who have suffered from it. Manic depression has two distinct sides—the depressive state and the manic state. People who suffer from manic depression experience a high commonly characterized by a sense of grandiosity, optimism, reduced need for sleep or food, irritability, delusional thinking, and hyperactivity. A period of more or less severe depression follows this "high" or mania. There are also more moderate manic states marked by tremendous creativity and productivity. A period of fatigue and indifference commonly follows. Manic depression is highly treatable.

Cyclothymia

Cyclothymia is a milder form of manic depression. Mild forms of mania alternate with mild bouts of depression. The symptoms are much less severe than full-blown bipolar illness. Instability in professional and personal relationships due to unpredictable moods and irritability, make those who suffer with cyclothymia difficult to live with and depend on. The cycles of cyclothymia are far shorter than in manic-depression and cyclothymics often do not seek treatment. They are extremely productive when they are in their hypomanic mode.

Post-partum depression

Due to the rapid change in hormonal levels after childbirth as well as the stress associated with the event and other factors, most women experience some type of emotional disturbance after giving birth; this can include grief, tearfulness, irritability, and a clinging dependence. In some cases these "baby blues" take on a life of their own, lasting weeks, months, and even years, and include anxiety and panic, and in some cases psychotic features and delusions. Post-partum depression usually appears six to eight weeks after giving birth. Postpartum depression is a treatable illness.

Seasonal affective disorder (SAD)

Those who suffer with season affective disorder tend to become depressed during a particular time of the year, most commonly during the autumn or winter seasons (beginning in October or November and lasting until April or May). During this time, those with SAD suffer altered sleep patterns, increased fatigue, apathy, irritability, and increased appetite. It is important for the person with SAD to get as much natural light as possible. Researchers have also uncovered a form of summer depression triggered by severe heat or intense light. This form of depressions occurs from June to August, but may be part of other depressive disorders as well.

Existential depression

Existential depression is brought on by a crisis of meaning or purpose. Transitions, a change of role at work, and a renewed sense or questioning of the larger meaning of life may trigger an existential depression. A number of researchers believe that a person's depression often has a connection to a lack of success in finding his or her passion in life, a connection to their deep inner wellspring of life.

Mood disorders related to a medical condition

Certain medical conditions can co-occur with clinical depression. These include endocrine conditions, neurological disorders, epilepsy, diseases that cause structural damage to the brain, viral infections, rheumatoid arthritis, lupus, vitamin deficiencies, heart disease, stroke, cancer, diabetes, multiple sclerosis, and others.

Medication-induced depression

A number of common prescription drugs have side effects that can induce depression. Some of these include cardiac drugs, sedatives, steroids, stimulants, antibiotics analgesics, and antifungal drugs. Ask your doctor if you suspect that medication you are taking could be a cause for depression.

Substance-induced mood disorder

Those who are depressed are more likely to use alcohol and other drugs to feel better, and those who use alcohol and other drugs are more likely to develop depression. During treatment, both the depression and the chemical dependency are treated.

_⁊ 7 ⁊_

"I'm Going Crazy!"

"There are so many voices in my head. Lord, which one is yours?" *Sean*

"I found that when I am having obsessive thoughts of guilt pounding in my head I frequently repeat, 'Jesus, I trust in you' and seek counsel especially through the sacrament of reconciliation. Jesus' mercy is far greater than anything I can do. I also find turning to Mary with the Hail Mary or the *Memorare* has brought peace to my mind and heart many, many times." *Linda Rose*

When someone says, "I'm going crazy!" the emphasis is nearly always on the last word: *crazy*. What does "crazy" feel like? For me crazy feels as if my mind's on overload and there are thunderstorms in my head, or being overwhelmed by little things and wanting to sit on the curb and cry. For each of us "crazy" feels a little different and we could no doubt speak for hours on how crazy we sometimes feel. Unfortunately, we too often pass over the subject of the sentence: "I." "*I* am going crazy!" This "I" is a very important word that denotes *ourselves*. Who is this *self*?

I Am the Home of the Trinity

At the outset of our pilgrimage on earth as Christians—whether it began when we were infants or later—we were washed in Baptism. The waters are the physical, visible expression of Christ who died and then resurrected. All Catholics were submerged into these baptismal waters and, at that moment, came into direct contact with Christ who has died and risen from the dead. When the person to be baptized is submerged under the water (or the water is poured on their forehead), they die and are buried with Christ. As the person rises from the water, they rise with Christ to new life. Of course, all we often see, if we attend a Baptism ceremony, is a few drops of water poured on the baby's forehead, and we hear the words, "I baptize you in the name of the Father, and of the Son, and of the Holy Spirit." We often are not aware of what is truly happening. At the moment of Baptism, Christ's death and resurrection penetrates the one being baptized. The water puts the person into direct contact with the Lord. All of the salvific power of the death and resurrection of Christ come together and are engraved within each person, because Jesus himself lives in us now. It is true. It is real.

At this precise moment, there is a total transformation. Sin and evil can no longer dominate us, because within us is the One who conquers evil; the One who took all sin, all tears, all sickness, all evil upon himself. Baptism transforms the entire being of the person. You become nothing less than the home of the Holy Trinity, the temple of the Holy Trinity, inhabited by the Most High God. You are the sanctuary, the living "temple," and all of

> *"Put on your jumping shoes and jump into the heart of God."*
> Meister Eckhart

heaven is within you! This is so real that the Fathers of the Church would quietly enter a church where the sacrament of Baptism was being celebrated, and then kneel before the newly baptized child. Inevitably, they would be asked, "Why are you doing this?" And they would answer that they were "adoring the Holy Trinity who has come to live within this child." They had the eyes of faith to see the reality of the grace of the sacrament.

Christ is the Victorious One who in his death and resurrection conquered evil. Death, sin, unhappiness, and destruction cannot have the last word. The last word is the victory of Christ and his triumph and fullness. No longer is there death that cannot bring life, pain that cannot generate fullness, sadness that we cannot convert into profound joy. There are no limitations, fragilities, psychological pain, or mood disorders stronger than the Resurrected One. We are children of the victory of the resurrection. If only this truth burned within us!

For years, I spent my Christmas Eve Masses and Easter vespers in tears, because I felt disconnected with the mystery of love. Now the tears I shed are tears of peace, knowing I can trust absolutely that the God, who is Love, loves me. If we have faith, if we keep loving and hoping through the tears, the joy of the resurrection, the glory of the God who is with us, will transform our tears into a calm and radiant certainty of God's love. Though now we cannot see the ultimate victory—on this earth we still live in a vale of tears, and unhappiness and sadness are part of our human reality—it will not remain the last word because we are with Someone who has already conquered death and pain. All pain he has transformed into victory. This is our faith. This is our truest certainty.

What Drives Us Crazy!

Distorted thought patterns are part of what makes us think we are going crazy. When a person is depressed, it seems that they can only focus on themselves, on surviving through each day. Depression can have disastrous effects on the quality of a person's life and contribute to the lowering of his or her self-esteem.

Stewart is successful in his career, but is often plagued by very dark thoughts when he is depressed. His job demands that he be in the public eye and so he can't indulge in melancholy feelings for very long. When he is feeling particularly down, or he finds his mind filled with depressed thoughts, he stops to look for the cause and then turns to a prayer of trust and hope a friend suggested to him long ago, "Jesus, here, you take this. You are greater than all these thoughts and feelings." He repeats this prayer calmly, and says, "It comforts me to know that I am turning moments of difficulty into acts of trust and hope through this prayer."

Unlike an ulcer, depression is usually not a "private" illness or a passing medical condition, such as chicken pox. Depressed people feel stigmatized by their illness, which they may be unable to completely control. They frequently face long-term behavior issues associated with their illness. Some depressed people suffer self-loathing, others may fear interacting with peers, and still others may feel their struggle with depression has weakened their credibility. Guilt and shame can cause a person to withdraw from situations that require interaction with others. Some feel that there's something wrong with them, different about them, and that everyone can see it. Sometimes we aren't even aware of how distorted our perceptions have become.

People who experience depression can be plagued by obsessive, irrational thoughts. These intrusive, repetitive thoughts are unrealistic and anxiety provoking. Most of us have to deal with a certain amount of this distorted negative thinking, but those with mood disorders can find it particularly crippling.

Listed below are twelve common distortions or faulty thought patterns, which are easily identified because they cause other painful emotions (such as worry and anxiety), and can be the cause of ongoing conflicts with other people.

All-or-nothing thinking: Everything in life becomes an all or nothing, black and white situation.

There is no in-between, no room for mistakes. *I did not receive the promotion I desired, so I must be a total failure and will never be promoted in my life.*

Overgeneralization: Broad, generalized conclusions are reached based on just one piece of evidence. *My new friend didn't invite me out to dinner; no one could ever really like me or want me as a friend.*

Catastrophizing: Everything, no matter how small, becomes a catastrophe. *I have a stomachache; it must be an ulcer.*

Control fallacies: A feeling that everything in life is controlled by an outside force or that you are responsible for everything. *I can't possibly leave the office on time. The place would fall apart without the work I do at night.*

Personalization: Interpreting everything as reflecting on you and your self-worth. *I know everyone in the office noticed the stain on my tie. They must all think I'm a jerk.*

Fallacies of fairness: Judging people's actions according to preconceived ideas of what is fair, right, and just. *If my children really cared about me, they'd come to dinner on time.*

Emotional reasoning: Believing that everything that you feel is true. *I feel ugly, therefore I am ugly.*

Demanding change: Deciding that a situation would improve if someone else changed according to my plans, so that my happiness depends on their changing. *If only my wife understood me better, we wouldn't argue as much.*

Labeling: Making a broad judgment based on one experience. *My secretary failed to catch a misspelling; either she doesn't know English or doesn't care about doing a good job and deserves to be fired.*

"Should" statements: Seeing life and behavior through a set of indisputable rules about how everyone should act. *I should never get angry or argue.*

Magnification and minimization: Discounting the good and magnifying the bad. *I couldn't answer one question after an impeccable presentation. Everyone congratulates me on the wonderful job, but I apologize profusely for my failure to respond to one question.*

Mind Reading: Basing assumptions and conclusions on what you think the other person is thinking. *The office manager passed my desk three times this morning. She must be checking up on me because she thinks I'm not doing my job.*

All of us have a steady diet of one or more of these distorted thought patterns. A good self-help book will offer rational correctives to these distortions. Most of these books teach you how to recognize your own negative thought patterns and the emotions that accompany them in order to substitute truthful thoughts that bring peace. For example, instead of thinking, "I am useless," which only makes you feel more depressed, you might learn to realize, "I am a hard worker when I feel well. At this moment I must be gentle with myself and trust in God's help."

For now, however, consider two or three of the above distortions you recognize in your own thinking.

In a quiet moment, sit down with Jesus. Talk to him about each of these distortions. Are they wreaking any havoc in your life, in your relationships, in your work? Do you have any new insights into what is happening in your life? Let Jesus speak about them from his perspective. Write down what he says. Write down one thing you would want to say back to him.

We spend 90 percent of our time dwelling upon the negative in our life, which, in reality, is only a fraction of our life's experiences. We only spend 10 percent of our time celebrating the positive and beautiful, the achievements and surprises, and our fulfilled desires. Start to turn that ratio around by adding a special time of gratitude into your week. Determine a length of time that is realistic for you. Make that time sacred so nothing else squeezes it out of your schedule. Spend your "gratitude time" thanking God for the good experiences, surprises, and beautiful things that happened during the week. Continue this practice and you will gradually find that your mind reflects fewer distortions and more reality.

> *"Let nothing disturb you, let nothing frighten you. Everything is changing. God alone is changeless."*
> Saint Teresa of Avila

Suggestion for prayer

These Stations of the Cross can be prayed when you feel yourself caught up in a negative distortion of your reality. The traditional fourteen stations can be replaced by other "stops" along the *Via Crucis*. These particular Stations include a reflection and prayer that highlights one of the cognitive distortions reviewed in this chapter. You can use this Way of the Cross as a time to unite the suffering you experience with the suffering of Jesus. ౪

FIRST STATION
Jesus in the Garden of Gethsemane

Jesus, when situations seem either a complete success or a devastating failure, help me to find the mystery of the "in-between" where failures are successes, and some successes are partly failures. You redeemed us and gained for us eternal life through what seemed your failure on the cross. Jesus, in my moments of agony, may I feel you so near to me, as a comfort and guide. ౪

SECOND STATION
Betrayed by Judas Jesus Is Arrested

Jesus, when I feel let down by people I have trusted or don't understand what someone's words or actions mean, give me the courage to ask for clarifications and explanations, instead of making generalized conclusions on just one piece of evidence. Teach me to respect the mystery of the other person whom I feel has hurt me, as you maintained your respect for Judas until the end. Jesus, when my moods start plummeting because of something another says or does, hold me in your arms. ☙

THIRD STATION
Jesus Is Condemned by the Sanhedrin

Jesus, help me keep the big things big, but most especially help me keep all the little things in my life *little*. When everything seems to be turning into a catastrophe, I want to remember you standing before the Sanhedrin with self-respect, trusting that your Father was going to take care of you. Jesus, when the world seems like it is spinning out of control, remind me of *our* Father's care. ☙

FOURTH STATION
Jesus Is Denied by Peter

Jesus, help me to realize there are things that are out of my control, and that no matter how hard I try, I cannot make everything perfect. Help me to enter the mystery of powerlessness, the moment when your handpicked apostle denied that he even knew you, and left you to die alone. Did you wonder why you had worked so hard to teach this man, who, in the end, denied you? Or did you hand the future of your kingdom over to God, since your death meant the giving up of all control? Jesus, when I think I am in control, gently pry open my hands and help me let go. Teach me to laugh and play again. ∾

FIFTH STATION
Jesus Is Judged by Pilate

Jesus, stand beside me when I feel like others are judging me or putting me down. Did you feel embarrassed when you were condemned in front of all those people? I feel like that sometimes. I interpret people's comments, even the way they look at me, as a condemnation or ridicule. Jesus, when I feel like everyone's looking at me, hide me in the shelter of your love. ∾

SIXTH STATION
Jesus Is Scourged and Crowned with Thorns

Jesus, this was so unfair. What were you thinking while the soldiers scourged you and then made fun of you, crowning you with thorns, and mocking you as a king? I'd be angry with them for making a fool of me. But you saw the larger picture; you knew life isn't all about fairness, that sometimes others will treat us unjustly. Jesus, when I don't think that others are treating me fairly, help me to remember that neither were you, that you walked this road ahead of me, that in the mystery of suffering I can unite my suffering to yours and share in the work of salvation with you. ∾

SEVENTH STATION
Jesus Bears the Cross

Jesus, when you started out through the crowded streets of Jerusalem toward Calvary, what did you feel about yourself? After all that had happened to you, were you wondering if maybe you had been wrong? Maybe if you had done things a different way, you wouldn't have ended up a man condemned to die as a criminal? Were you afraid as the people bustled around you, trying to stay clear of the soldiers? Sometimes I feel negative about myself. I carry my cross of depression and I think I'm no good, a failure, and ugly. Jesus, when I feel this way about myself, help me to remember that it isn't true. Help me to carry my cross beside you, to look into your eyes, and there see who I truly am in your eyes, which always look on me with love. ໑

EIGHTH STATION
Jesus Is Helped by Simon the Cyrenian to Carry the Cross

Jesus, did you hope that someone would help you carry the cross, or were you surprised that the Roman soldiers asked Simon to take your cross on his own shoulders? Many times, I expect or demand a Simon to appear, for someone to change their attitude and help me out a little. When my Simon doesn't appear, Lord, you be my Simon, and don't let me become bitter and blame everyone else for my problems. Jesus, let me see your face, and I shall be saved. ❧

NINTH STATION
Jesus Meets the Women of Jerusalem

Jesus, the women were so compassionate. What did they see in you? It would have been so easy for you to curse the entire human race for the treatment you received. But you didn't fall into the trap of labeling everyone because of some people's actions. You were still open to accept the kindnesses those women showed you. When I make broad judgments because of the actions of a few, send me someone like the women on the road to Calvary to remind me of the beauty of life and the ultimate reliability of love. ❧

TENTH STATION
Jesus Is Crucified

Jesus, if you wanted to, you could have had the last word. You could have justified yourself, proven to everyone around your cross that you really were God's Son. "Come down off your cross and we'll believe," they taunted. You could have done that. Jesus, I find it so hard not to have the last word, especially when I *am* right. Jesus Truth, may I trust that the truth will always come out in the end. That it is not justifying myself with others that matters, but being in right relationship with you, with myself, and with others that ultimately counts. ❧

ELEVENTH STATION
Jesus Promises His Kingdom to the Good Thief

The good thief had a lot of nerve to trust you in those last moments before his death. You could have told him that he should never have broken the law in the first place. You could have "given him a sermon." But you didn't. You saw that life is about more than rules, though they have their place. Life is about reconciliation and acceptance, and love that creates goodness around itself. When I use "should" statements with others, or myself, teach me the mystery of creative love that can promise eternal happiness to repentant criminals. ❧

TWELFTH STATION
Jesus Speaks to His Mother and the Disciple

It must have been hard for Mary to stand beneath the cross. People who wanted to see you dead surrounded Mary. She saw the child she had cradled in her arms stretched beyond recognition on the arms of the cross. She heard you promising the good thief eternal happiness in your kingdom. She received the charge of caring for John as a son. Truly, beneath the cross all of us became her children. Mary was able to hold the beauty and the pain of those last hours of your life together, neither lashing out in anger nor discounting the good. Jesus, entrust me again to such a wonderful mother, that I might neither discount the good in and around me nor magnify the bad. Mary, be my sure hope. ᘐ

THIRTEENTH STATION
Jesus Dies on the Cross

Jesus, no one knew your final thoughts as you died. There are the traditional "seven last words" recorded in the Gospels, but I wonder what else you were thinking. Did you think of me? Sometimes I think I'm a mind reader and am suspicious of other people's attitudes toward me. But I never have to be afraid of what you think of me, because you can only love and create love all around you. Jesus, help me believe in your love. ᘐ

FOURTEENTH STATION
Jesus Is Buried in the Tomb

I can imagine all of nature in mourning when you, my Jesus, were buried in the tomb, as if all living things cradled your sacred, life-less body. Jesus, I am never alone. I am cradled in your Father's arms, held by the universe, connected in the web of life and history with every other human person who has ever lived on this planet. And now I can feel

how all creation groans and waits for *my* resurrection, for the moment of exaltation when
tears will be no more and sorrow will be
wiped away. Jesus, resurrected Lord and
Savior, be my salvation. ☙ Amen.

☙ ✺ ☙

For one who is depressed

Find a piece of music or art that helps you
visualize and feel the presence of God within
you. If it is a piece of art, place it in a prominent place in your room where you will see it
every day. If it is a particular piece of music,
play it often, especially when you are down.

For a friend

Try to find a way to celebrate your friend as
a temple of God. It could be as simple as being
more supportive and respectful. Or you might
want to send small Christian note-cards or e-
mail messages.

Getting a Grip on Obsessive, Unrealistic Thinking

Those suffering with depression struggle with negative, irrational, obsessive thoughts. These thoughts not

only make everything a "big deal" or a "catastrophe," they also may make it difficult to believe God loves you—or anyone else for that matter. They can make you question if life has any meaning, or if you are alone and abandoned in the universe. Though these dark thoughts begin to lighten as the depression lifts, you can form a habit of "truthful" thinking by confronting such thoughts and by using mantras, repeated short prayers. Below are guidelines for changing these thoughts as well as some different mantras you could choose to pray. One may strike you as something you may wish to always say, or you may wish to alternate them on different days or according to your varying moods. The more you occupy your mind with thoughts that purify and strengthen, the less power depressive thoughts will have over you. Some are traditional, some represent newer ways of approaching God, and finally some of them have been suggested to me and I have found them helpful in counteracting obsessive negative and "shaming" self-talk.

Basic Guidelines for Changing Irrational Thoughts:

Evaluate the demand or the statement. (e.g., 1. You *should* do this. "Do I really want to do this? Is it really in my best interests to do this?" 2. What if this happens? "It hasn't happened yet. What are the realistic probabilities that it will?")

Take off the pressure. (e.g., 1. I'm allowed to say "No." If I say yes, there is no hurry and it won't be terrible if I find I have to change my mind. 2. If this happens it will be painful or frustrating, but it won't be terrible or catastrophic.)

Make a plan. (e.g., 1. Set small, realistic goals. Pace yourself. 2. Consider whether or not there is anything you can do to prevent the negative event from happening. If so, do it. If not, accept that you can't.)

Mantras for Finding Peace and Truth

Lord Jesus Christ, have mercy on me (the Jesus Prayer).

Jesus.

Spirit of Jesus, let me hear your gentle voice (Frances Libermann).

Lord, I am the apple of your eye (Rev. Jack Tackney).

I have caught sight of you, my Love, and you are very beautiful (Kathryn J. Hermes, FSP).

My hope is in the Beloved, my strength and my joy (Nan C. Merrill).

May it be done to me as you have said (Mary, Mother of God).

In my heart, O Lord, I treasure your promises (Psalm 119).

I believe that God is love, that God holds us and saves us (St. Edith Stein).

_ᥕ 8 ᥕ_

Start Humming in the Darkness

"O guiding night! O night more lovely than the dawn! O night that has united the Lover with his beloved, transforming the beloved in her Lover." *St. John of the Cross*

"One of the things I've found the most difficult suffering from depression is getting through times of prayer. It can be nearly impossible to sit silently focused for any length of time without a gnawing anxiety growing inside me or the invasion of unpleasant memories or thoughts. At such times I find it useful to practice the prayer of presence, staying at prayer only as long as I can remain so peacefully. Quietly I am aware of God's presence inside me, around me, with me. I am present to God. I love God and I know God loves me. This prayer doesn't demand anything else. No great thoughts or overwhelming emotions are necessary." *MaryJo*

St. John Vianney, the famous Curé of the tiny French village of Ars, is most popularly known as the holy and humble priest who spent sixteen to eighteen hours a day hearing confessions and giving advice to long processions of people. He practiced extraordinary penances and fasts for the conversion of sinners and was subject to diabolic persecution all his priestly life. It is said that the devil revealed once that if there were but three priests in the world like the Curé of Ars, the devil would lose his kingdom.

"You need not cry very loud; God is nearer to us than we think."
Brother Lawrence

What is less known is the overwhelming depression that weighed upon John Vianney's soul without relief his entire life. Though he was the most sought after man in all of France he seemed incapable of seeing the immense amount of good he was doing. Despite the tens of thousands of pilgrims who traveled to Ars each year in the hope of receiving the sacraments or a word of advice from him, he believed himself useless. The priest who had reawakened the faith of a village and set all France aflame through his preaching and holiness felt God so far from him that he was afraid he had no more faith. He believed himself to have no intelligence or gift of discernment. It is as if God drew a veil over his eyes so that he could see nothing of what God was doing through him for others. The Curé feared he was ruining everything and had become an obstacle in God's way.

The root of John Vianney's severe depression was his fear of doing badly at every turn, and the thousands who traveled to Ars increased his terror. It never occurred to him that he might have a special grace. Instead, he feared that the long line of penitents to his village church were a sign that he was a hypocrite. He feared facing the judgment with the responsibility for all these people on his conscience. There was not a moment when he felt that God was satisfied with him. A great and profound sadness possessed his soul so powerfully that he eventually could not even imagine relief.

Whenever the tempests of depression seemed to have enough power to drown him in the vision of his own miseries, the Curé would bow his head, throw himself before God like "a dog at the feet of his master," and allow the storm to pass without changing his resolve to love and serve God if he could. Yet he kept this pain so private that except for a few confidantes, most people saw only tranquility and gentleness in his bearing.

Jesus Is in the Darkness with You

You may discover that the shadows and tempests of depression alter the way you look at God and the way you believe God looks at you. When you pray you may be unable to sit still or to keep your mind focused for more than a few moments. Everything may appear to be a huge gaping hole of silence, all so useless. God may seem to be mocking your attempts to pray. I know people who have gone three, five, ten years without "praying," though they were faithful to setting time aside for prayer regardless of its seeming uselessness. In the haunting darkness where all communication had gone silent, they found loneliness, boredom, frustration, anger. Were they praying? Yes.

"Praying the Rosary remained a great help to me during my worse times of depression," Joseph, an employee of a large chain of bookstores, said. "I acquired books that had various mysteries of the Rosary, Eucharistic mysteries, Marian mysteries, Passion mysteries, Holy Spirit mysteries.... It gave me a lot of variety, and that helped me to keep focused on prayer and remain somewhat calm. It instilled some peace and quiet in my heart."

"Live in faith and hope, though it be in darkness. Cast your care on God."

St. John of the Cross

Recognizing agony in a void that is filled only with darkness and absence calls a depressed person to be present to the Now, even if the Now is darkness. There is a God in that void, the God of Jesus. To be present to this God, to know that Jesus is in the darkness *with* you and *for* you *is* prayer, even were no words or act of love to pass through your heart. God's abiding love is deep within, never forsaking you in darkness. You are alone in the void with the Son of God—both of you keeping silent. Suffering with you is Jesus, the abandoned Son on the cross. When it is impossible to hold on to a thought or to pray, Jesus is praying and contemplating within the one who is suffering from depression. Day by day, moment by moment, groping in the darkness, you are not alone. Jesus is struggling with you. He is there feeling it all. Nothing goes unnoticed by him or his Father. Through Jesus' Spirit who is in you, you can hope for peace.

Ideas for Praying When Depressed

St. Gregory Nazianzus wrote these words during a time when he found anxiety and depression crowding out any space for prayer in his soul:

The breath of life, O Lord, seems spent.
My body is tense, my mind filled with anxiety,
yet I have no zest, no energy.
I am helpless to allay my fears.
I am incapable of relaxing my limbs.
Dark thoughts constantly invade my head....
Lord, raise up my soul, revive my body.

If this is happening to you, try these forms of prayer and contemplative love:

1. *Try to find a quiet place.* Put on some soothing music. Keep it soft and gentle. Take a few deep breaths, holding each one for a few seconds and then slowly exhaling. Relax. Feel the chair you're sitting on, your feet on the floor. Smell the scents in the room. Imagine Jesus coming toward you with a smile on his face. Tell him how you are feeling right now—anxious, uncomfortable, fidgety, distracted, wanting to focus. Tell him what things are like for you today. Open your heart to him. Feel his presence very close to you. Let his love into your heart. Thank him for this gift.

2. *Go for a walk. Take some pleasant music with you.* As you go, notice the sky, feel the season. Recognize what is around you. Feel at home right now. Offer your heart to Jesus, even if your pain is deep. Though you may be alone on your walk, Jesus is in

your heart. Tell him what you see...the beauty around you. Tell him how you feel...even if it is dark. Remember he wants you to tell him everything in your life...joys and pains.

3. *Call to mind someone else you know who is hurting or sick.* Focus for a few minutes on what that person may be feeling, and on what you would like to say to him or her. Lift this person up by name to Jesus and ask his blessing on them.

4. *Hold a crucifix in your hands.* Close your eyes and think of Jesus in agony. Join your sufferings to his in his act of redemption.

5. *If you're feeling low, go to a quiet place and hold your Bible.* Read Psalm 130 or focus on a phrase of it. Embrace how you feel, even if it's uncomfortable. Know that God is loving you through these moments of darkness.

6. *When you are unable to focus because your mind is racing, try to remember and pray the words, "My God, I love you."* Open yourself to God's love.

7. *Turn on soft music.* Read this Bible verse over and over while thinking about it: "My God, my God, why have you forgotten me?" (cf. Mk 15:34). This is Jesus' own prayer of emptiness and abandonment.

8. *When you pass by your local church, stop in for a few minutes.* Pause and connect with the One who loves you.

9. *If you can't get up, lie still and repeat the name of Jesus over, and over, and over.* His love catches these words and he embraces you with love.

10. *Go to Eucharistic adoration and spend some time in God's presence.*

Where God Is

Sr. Thomas Halpin was diagnosed with bipolar disorder when she was thirty-eight. In one way, it was a relief for her to have an explanation for her psychotic episodes and suicidal thoughts. In another way, she felt that her life had come apart. Since she had often shared with me, I knew some of her story, but very few knew what her life had become. When I asked her how she kept praying through those years she said quite honestly, "I didn't think I was praying, but I had made a commitment to pray. I was convinced that Jesus was present in the Eucharist. I felt like I 'owed him time.' So I would just go to church and sit. Sometimes I even deliberately ignored God. I was so angry. Before my illness, I had been able to accomplish so much, and here I was, reduced to nothing. I thought God had played a dirty trick on me. It was this way for six or seven years.

"I complained on and on about what God had done to me, through session after session with my therapist. Finally, he said to me, 'Go home and think of all the things you have to be grateful for.' I left his office very angry. Who was he to tell me that? Later when I went to chapel, I stared at the tabernacle and started thinking. I saw faces. I saw my therapist. I saw the faces of my sisters. And I heard, 'This is where I am. You've been missing me, and I've been here the whole time. You won't find me in a vision or a miracle. Because this is how I choose to work—through others and only through others.' That reflection made me realize more and more the personal investment God has in me and I have in him. It's been twelve years now. I can talk to God easily. And now, I'm able to talk about love."

Sr. Thomas was faithful to a contemplative silence. Almost imperceptibly through the years something seemed to change, beautifully, as the dark sky changes during a sunrise. Sr. Thomas now has a strength, a depth, a compassion, a heart, a kind of prayer found in few people. She had experienced a mystery in the life of Christ that many people never will. She had suffered Jesus' passion to the bitter end, and she had been resurrected more gloriously.

––––––––

Suggestion for prayer

Create a prayer corner or a quiet place in your home. Put in it strong visual reminders of God, Mary, or a favorite saint: a crucifix, icon, picture, or statue. Keep one or two CD's of instrumental, praise and worship, or other favorite music handy to help set the mood or create an atmosphere in which you can sense God's presence and allow God to minister to you in your need. Incense sticks or small candles are strong sensory elements that can also help arrest depressive thoughts. When we cannot pray with words, simply watching a candle flame dancing in the darkness can help us enter into a contemplative peace. As you find motivational quotes, write them out and keep them in your prayer corner. Place there whatever else helps you lift up your mind and heart, and find peace and hope in prayer. God does not demand things of you in your prayer. God wants to give you so many gifts when you open your heart to him. Use whatever helps you open up in trust.

◦◦ ❈ ◦◦

For one who is depressed

Try to reflect on what it is like for you to pray. How would you like God to be there for you? Share this with God.

For a friend

Read a biography or autobiography of someone who has suffered depression or manic-depression. Some suggestions are: *An Unquiet Mind,* or *Touched by Fire: Manic-Depressive Illness and the Artistic Temperament,* both by Kay Redfield Jamison; *The Depression Workbook Second Edition: A Guide for Living with Depression and Manic Depression,* by M. A. Copeland, et al; *Depression Fallout: The Impact of Depression on Couples and What You Can Do to Preserve the Bond,* by Anne Sheffield; *The Noonday Demon: An Atlas of Depression,* by Andrew Solomon; *A Brilliant Madness: Living with Manic-Depressive Illness,* by Patty Duke, et al.

Healing Scriptures

The Scriptures contain the words God speaks to us. Find those passages that speak to you in a particularly strong way of God's love. Repeat these words often. Personalize them with your name, for they are a word truly addressed to you.

_____, "you are precious in my sight" (Is 43:4).

_____, "I am the light of the world, you are the light of the world" (Jn.8:12; Mt 5:14).

_____, "I have called you by name, you are mine" (Is 43:1).

_____, "your grief will turn to joy" (Jn 16:20).

_____, "the Lord your God is your light" (Rev 22:5).

_____, "live on in me, as I do in you" (Jn 15:4).

_____, "cast all your cares on God, who cares for you" (1 Pt 5:7).

_✑ **9** ✑_

"Don't Look the Other Way"

"Before I used to go out and have a great time with my friends. Now they never invite my anywhere. I don't think they know what to say to me." *Caitlyn*

"One day a co-worker scolded me, 'You have taken long enough to work through whatever you need to work through. Get over it!' I was shocked, but I had the courage to stand up for myself and respond, 'Have I changed?' 'Well, yes,' she responded. 'Okay, then.' Everything has its own rhythm and healing does too. There is no timetable to keep, no right or wrong amount of time needed for healing." *Jeanine*

There is one thing worse than suffering depression, and that is suffering depression alone. There are many reasons why we might shy away from people who are suffering depression. We may honestly not know what to

"Why is it that all men who are outstanding in philosophy, poetry, or the arts are melancholic?"
Aristotle

say. Our attempts to solve another's problem may be met with frustration and defensiveness on the part of the person suffering with depression. Not knowing what to do to help can make us feel awkward and helpless. In frustration, we may decide that if the person suffering depression isn't going to get on with life, they'll just have to go on by themselves. Gradually, without really intending it, the depressed person is marginalized and soon forgotten.

Maintaining a concerned friendship with someone suffering with depression requires that we face the fact that we can't fix the situation any more than he or she can. Both sides have to learn the lesson of God's divine love. God came to companion us in our suffering by coming into our midst. In Christ, God learned what our suffering was like. God didn't tell us what to do to fix this suffering or show us how to sidestep it. He drew near to us. He suffered with and for us. He died in darkness, powerlessness, and abandonment to destroy the power of sin and evil which held us captive, but he didn't take evil away and we still feel its consequences. God's divine love follows the dynamic of the cross.

When we draw near to companion someone who is suffering from depression, we too are drawn into this divine dynamic of "compassioning." The first thing we learn when we companion someone who is suffering with depression is that all survival, organizational, and problem-solving skills that work so well in other areas of our life have no place in this friendship. Only the dynamics of companioning, of being with, of suffering alongside another, as God has done for us in Christ, are operative here. Suffering makes both the one who is depressed as well as his or her friend feel very poor.

The poverty of depression offers another lesson of divine love. God revealed his glory in the broken body of his crucified Son. And still today, God's glory is revealed in vulnerability and brokenness. We sometimes erroneously think that God's glory is only apparent in magnificent cathedrals and great works of charity. But the cross—as God's choice for displaying his wisdom and power—shows us that God's glory is actually most evident in quiet, anguished suffering, such as the one suffering with depression is sharing with his or her friend. The one who reaches out a hand in friendship begins to learn vulnerability and the poverty of powerlessness. But he or she will one day touch the presence of God in their friend.

Finally, a concerned person who consistently reaches out to a depressed friend comes to know the blessing of being trusted. Over time, both learn to rest in their poverty, discarding all pretenses. Both are able to offer to and receive from one another. The paradoxical outcome of all this is that the friend discovers that he or she has received more than what he or she had given.

The Five Beatitudes of Companioning a Depressed Friend

Blessed are they who tear up labels.

When you have decided to begin or continue a friendship with someone who is suffering from depression, especially if he or she has been struggling with chronic or clinical depression for many years, it is easy to unconsciously assume a patronizing attitude: this "poor person" needs my help. If you think your friend is lucky to have you to help them, throw that idea out before you even start. Such a friendship will end in frustration and anger on both sides, because your friendship is with the person's illness, not with him or her as a person. You have already classified or "branded" your friend with a label. I am convinced that we hold many people hostage in cages made of labels for their entire lives. A label can destroy a person's future.

Likewise, in a Christian community there is no place for labels, because there are no labels in the Gospels. In fact, Jesus scandalized the religious leaders of his day because he ate and drank with those who had been labeled "publicans and sinners" by the religious institution. Jesus' radical ideas of evangelical friendship were rooted in the heart of God "whose sun shines on the good and the bad" (Mt 5:45), and "who loved the world so much that he sent his Son into the world to be its salvation" (cf. Jn 3:16). Jesus had no patience with labels, and neither should we.

To break open the cages in which you may subtly be locking yourself or a friend suffering from a depression, it may be helpful to discover some famous people who have suffered or suffer from a mood disorder and yet have had a tremendous effect on the world.

Here are just a few:

Authors: Hans Christian Andersen, Arthur Benson, F. Scott Fitzgerald, Graham Greene, Ernest Hemingway, William James, Ralph Waldo Emerson, Herman Melville, Eugene O'Neill, Jean Stafford, Mary Shelley, Leo Tolstoy, Mary Wollstonecraft, Tennessee Williams, and Virginia Wolf.

Poets: Charles Baudelaire, William Blake, George Gordon (Lord Byron), Emily Dickenson, T. S. Eliot, Robert Fergusson, Thomas Gray, Gerard Manley Hopkins, Victor Hugo, John Keats, Mikhail Lermontov, James Russell Lowell, Edna St. Vincent Millay, Edgar Allan Poe, Ezra Pound, Anne Sexton, Delmore Schwartz, Lord Tennyson, Francis Thompson, and Walt Whitman.

Composers and Musicians: Samuel Barber, Ludwig van Beethoven, Anton Bruckner, Kurt Cobain, John Denver, Stephen Foster, George Frederic Handel, Gustav Holst, Charles Ives, Modest Mussorgsky, Robert Schumann, Peter Tchaikovsky, Hugo Wolf, and Bernd Alois Zimmerman.

Artists: Vincent van Gogh, George Innes, Ernst Ludwig Kirchner, Michelangelo, Dante Gabriel Rossetti.

Statesmen: Menachem Begin (Prime Minister of Israel, Nobel Laureate), Winston Churchill, Calvin Coolidge, Abraham Lincoln, Richard M. Nixon.

Saints: St. John of the Cross, St. Thérèse of Lisieux, St. John Vianney, St. Benedict Joseph Labre, and St. Edith Stein.

Many people would be surprised to discover how many prominent and successful individuals today suffer from mood disorders. Among such individuals are: Roseanne Arnold, actor, writer, comedienne (also has Multiple personality disorder and obsessive compulsive disorder); Dick Cavett, writer, media personality; Tony Dow, actor, director; Kitty Dukakis, former first lady of Massachusetts; Patty Duke, actor, writer; Connie Francis, actor, musician; Peter Gabriel, musician; Charles Haley, athlete; Kristy McNichol, actor; Spike Mulligan, comic actor; Abigail Padgett, mystery writer; Murray Pezim, financier; Charley Pride, musician; Axl Rose, musician; William Styron, writer; James Taylor, musician; Mike Wallace, news anchor; Robin Williams, actor, comedian.

> *"We will suffer, and suffer with one another, but in doing so we will uncover nothing less than the presence of a God whose consolation keeps us going."*
>
> Henri Nouwen,
> *Turn My Mourning into Dancing*

It is unfortunate that we so often push aside those with depression, categorizing them as "useless," conveniently ignoring them, or patronizing them. We impoverish ourselves by not companioning and serving these great "poor ones."

Blessed are those who don't try to be a doctor.

One of the most important things a person suffering from depression needs is appropriate diagnosis and treatment. Encourage your friend to pursue professional medical care. A complete physical is essential for correct diagnosis. What looks like depression could be a symptom of an underlying organic problem. The person should make an appointment for an interview with a psychologist in order to determine their unique experience of depression. Is she suffering from generalized anxiety? Is he depressed because of a recent job loss? Is she exhibiting signs of post-traumatic stress, possibly indicative of traumatic events in her life?

Although you can't be your friend's doctor, you can encourage your friend to get professional help. You may need to encourage your friend to stay with the treatment until symptoms begin to abate, or to seek different treatment if no improvement occurs. Because each person's body chemistry is unique, the search for the medication or combination of medications that can help a person with depression can last over an extended period. It's essential to be persevering and patient. Encourage your friend to be hopeful and continue to try new medications as prescribed by his or her doctor until the right combination is found. Often once someone suffering from depression begins to pursue professional help, they immediately start to cut corners: "I don't really need to get all those tests"; "I think I know what the problem is, I don't need to go back to the doctor"; "I feel good now so I stopped taking my medicine." Cutting corners with depression always complicates the diagnostic process. Encourage them to stick with their treatment and to keep asking their doctor before making any major treatment decisions of their own.

You may be the only one with whom your friend shares what he or she is really feeling. This is an awesome trust. Welcome whatever he or she may wish to say to you without judging. Encourage your friend to share important information with his or her doctor.

Blessed are those who offer emotional support.

Depression can marginalize its sufferers so that they feel as if a door is quickly closing, shutting them off from the land of the living. But you can put your foot in the door to keep it open, even if just a crack. Call your friend. Send her e-mails or flowers. Invite him to go for walks, to the movies, or hiking. Invite your friend to go to Church with you or to join with you in your parish's activities. Take her along shopping, or ask him to accompany your family on a picnic. Pray with her over the phone. Send him e-mail promises of prayer and support. Offer diversion and company, but don't insist. Too many demands can increase feelings of failure.

Remember: your stable interest in your friend's welfare should not depend on any improvement on their part. Your fidelity lets her know she is accepted.

Your support lets him know that you believe in him. Your friend can learn from you how to accept him or herself, that life is good, that joy can eventually be experienced again.

Hans's sister Laura was extremely depressed. She had taken time off from work and stayed with her older sister because she was afraid to be alone. Hans lived on the other side of the country, but he made sure to call her once a week and write to her every two days. He remembers that he kept repeating to her that he loved her and Jesus loved her even more. Hans told her that he was praying for her and that he prayed that her guardian angel would protect her. Later, Hans said, his sister told him that it was the thought of her guardian angel being with her that had been her greatest comfort.

This type of a friendship can be tested in two ways. What if the person never seeks professional help or, even with medication and therapy, still does not seem to improve? What if your friend becomes angry with you, or accuses you of meddling in their affairs? Though you can encourage and be there for others, their decisions and journey are ultimately their own. God cares for them even more than you could ever care, and sometimes putting them in the hands of God is all—and actually the best thing—you can do. God has mysterious ways of saving each person. Your friend may never pursue wellness, and yet, in God's designs and their human weakness, they may be living an apostolate of suffering. The temptation to take control of your friend's situation is great, but he or she needs to be free to seek wholeness in his or her own way. Such situations call for tremendous patience and freedom to both hold your friend and let him or her go their chosen way.

Blessed are the compassionate.

If someone were to ask you if you thought of yourself as a compassionate person, you might reply yes, or at least, "I believe so." However, the true meaning of the word compassion is more than mere sympathy or pity. It comes from the Latin root to "suffer with." To show compassion means sharing in the suffering "passion" of another. In his book, *Never Forget,* Henri Nouwen wrote, "To live with compassion means to enter others' dark moments. It is to walk into places of pain, not to flinch or look away when another agonizes. It means to stay where people suffer. Compassion holds us back from quick, eager explanations when tragedy meets someone we know or love...." A lack of compassion often comes from the all too human rejection of suffering characteristic of our times. It is difficult to be truly compassionate.

Your journey of walking with someone in his or her pain begins with both compassionate and much respectful silence. Here are some compassionate words that you might say:

"I love you."

"I care."

"You're not alone in this."

"I'm not going to leave you."

"Do you want a hug?"

"You are important to me."

"We can ride this out together."

"When all this is over, I'll still be there and so will you."

"All I want to do now is give you a hug and a shoulder to cry on."

"You're not crazy."

"I can't imagine how hard this must be."

"I'm sorry you're going through this."

"I'm never going to say, 'I know how you feel' unless I truly do, but if I can do anything to help, I will."

Listed below are examples of uncompassionate words that should never be said to someone suffering with depression:

"It's all in your mind."

"I thought you were stronger than that."

"You have so many things to be thankful for."

"Happiness is a choice."

"Well at least it's not that bad."

"Get a grip."

"There are other people worse off than you."

"You are what you think."

"The only one you're hurting is yourself."

"Why don't you smile more?"

"You're always worried about your problems."

"Go have some fun for a change."

"I want the old you back. I don't like the way you are now."

"Maybe you need to trust God more."

"Just hang in there."

"You are your own worst enemy."

"My life isn't fun either."

"What's *your* problem?"

"Will you stop that constant whining?"

"Haven't you gotten tired of all this me-me-me stuff?"

Blessed are those who contemplate what God is doing.

Your friendship with someone who is depressed can become a new form of prayer. We spend most of our adult life analyzing and calculating. Neither of these, however, are building blocks of prayer. Prayer is about observing, contemplating, wondering, imagining. As you develop a friendship that leaves the other be, you may find the following suggestions helpful:

1. Remember occasions in which God has rescued you. Write them down. Offer gratitude to God for

them. Contemplate what God has done in your own life.

2. Before meeting with your friend, spend some time in silence. Relax. Be calm and serene. Tell God that you want to contemplate what God will be doing while you and your friend are together.

3. Thank God in your heart every time you realize God has been helping your friend, even if your friend cannot see it. You will begin to see that God will help your friend in God's own time. He has no timetable, no agenda. God is mystery. And so is your friend. Let God do the rescuing. You can count on God.

4. Pray for your friend.

5. Tell your friend you are praying for him or her. Occasionally point out what you see God is doing in your friend's life. *"It seems to me that God is letting you remember some beautiful times in your life when you felt loved by others." "You seem much more peaceful. God has given you a tremendous gift."*

Suggestion for prayer

Sacred Scripture is full of passages that offer comfort and examples of how to companion those who are suffering in any way. Through the people in the story of salvation history, we see the same human emotions and struggles we face—and God's unchanging love for us, and presence with us in every situation. Here are only a few of the many beautiful lines of Scripture for the friends of those with depression to contemplate.

———

As the sun was setting, all those who had any who were sick with various kinds of diseases brought them to him; and he laid his hands on each of them and cured them (Lk 4:40).

———

Then some people came [to Jesus], bringing to him a paralyzed man, carried by four of them. And when they could not bring him to Jesus because of the crowd, they removed the roof above him; and after having dug through it, they let down the mat on which the paralytic lay...[Jesus] said to the paralytic, "I say to you, stand up, take your mat and go to your home" (Mk 2:3–4, 11).

———

Come to me, all you that are weary and are carrying heavy burdens, and I will give you rest. Take my yoke upon you, and learn from me; for I am gentle and humble in heart, and you will find rest for your souls (Mt. 11:28).

———

Jesus prayed, "Father, if you are willing, remove this cup from me; yet, not my will but yours be done."

Then an angel from heaven appeared to him and gave him strength (Lk 22:42–43).

———————

Mary stood weeping outside the tomb. As she wept, she bent over to look into the tomb; and she saw two angels in white, sitting where the body of Jesus had been lying.... They said to her, "Woman, why are you weeping?"... She turned around and saw Jesus standing there.... Jesus said to her, "Woman why are you weeping? Whom are you looking for?" (Jn 20:11–13).

———— ✿ ————

For one who is depressed

Trusting friends is difficult when one is depressed. It takes a lot of energy to interact with others. It is a great risk to believe and to hope that another will welcome and care about you when life itself seems to have given up on you. For one week, keep a small notebook in your pocket or purse. Jot down the times that you wish someone cared and would be there for you, as well as any behaviors or choices on your part which are keeping such a friendship from developing. For example, not joining others because you feel they won't want you around. This self-defeating behavior perpetuates a situation of isolation and loneliness. At the end of the week, decide on one thing you can change in your own life that would make it possible for deeper friendships to blossom. As you begin to make changes in your life, what surprises you?

For a friend

After you speak with a friend suffering from depression, take a moment to jot down the things that you remember having said. Try to notice if you expected your friend to be better or do better because of what you were saying to him or her, or if you just relaxed and tried to show her or him God's love.

Four Tips If a Friend or Family Member Is Depressed

First: Inform yourself. Read as much as you can about depression. There is ample information available from medical institutions on the internet. Depression is a serious illness that requires professional attention. Depression isn't the result of a character flaw. It's not laziness. It's not simply a case of "the blues." People with depression aren't faking it and cannot "snap out of it."

Second: Express your concern by listening to your friend or family member if he or she wants to talk. Respect his or her desire for privacy if they would rather not talk. Asking how you can help lets your friend or family member know that you are willing to be supportive, even if he or she cannot suggest what you can do. Depressed people often feel worthless. Remind your friend or family member how much he or she means to you, and celebrate their strengths and successes. Encourage healthy behavior and activities. Invite your loved one to join you in activities or visiting family or mutual friends. But don't push and don't expect too much too soon.

Third: Direct the person to professional help. Convincing someone who's depressed that he or she has an illness and needs professional help may take time and patience. Gently explain why you're concerned, describing changes you've seen in his or her behavior and moods. Ask if something is going on and why he or she seems down. Offer to provide referrals or to go along for an appointment. You could also phone the doctor in advance of an appointment and share your observations, which could help in the diagnosis.

Fourth: Being a close friend or family member of someone who's depressed isn't easy. Make sure you take care of yourself, especially if you find yourself becoming angry or irritable, withdrawing from activities that used to bring you joy, or worrying excessively about the situation. Take care of yourself by: 1) enlisting help from other family members and friends; 2) understanding your own feelings or needs and expressing them respectfully to the person who is depressed (i.e., "I love you, but sometimes I need some time for myself"); 3) share your feelings with a trusted friend, family member, or pastoral minister at your parish; 4) reserve time for yourself, exercise, eat a healthy diet, and do things you enjoy.

～ 10 ～

Healings Are Not "Success Stories"

"There has got to be an end to this depression. I want to get on with my life and what I'm supposed to be." *Rad*

"During my first bout with depression, I made a novena in preparation for Christmas. With as much confidence as I could muster, I asked God to heal me—that was the Christmas gift I wanted. At Midnight Mass I went to Communion anticipating this gift. As Jesus and I conversed, he very gently asked me, 'Is it okay if I don't heal you today?' This was the first time I had been aware of God's gentleness, and his gentleness in asking me moved me deeply. What could I respond but 'okay'? I have to admit, however, that I was very disappointed. Sixteen years later, I am grateful that God did not heal me that Christmas (and am amazed that I can say this). I am a stronger person today. I am a courageous person today. Perhaps my life would have been easier, but I would not have grown into who I have become. Recently I did receive my Christmas gift. I am healed." *Sr. Marie*

There is something of the absurd about depression and other mood disorders, which often bestow great gifts on their victims even as their capacity to use them is limited. Medical literature will tell you many of those suffering from depression go on to live healthy and productive lives. There are miracles and many find healing after suffering a one-time bout with depression. For others, depression recurs seasonally. And some can never completely leave depression behind, though they have returned to a seemingly "normal life." However, if all you want to achieve is a return to a life like everyone else's, you content yourself with knowing only pale reflections of joy and sorrow, meaning, and love. Depression and mood disorders can be a vocation, a calling.

"The greatest blessing comes to us through madness."
Socrates

Annie is a 45-year-old woman who has suffered with chronic pain and resultant depression. She says of her experience: "Before I used to think that God could perform a miracle if he wanted to. Since he didn't, I thought I must be so awful that I wasn't worth his time. Now I see things differently. I am not cured, but Jesus has gifted me with the grace to really know that he is with me and that he loves me beyond measure. He has helped me to see that darkness and pain are not a sign of my being 'bad,' or that if I had just tried harder I would be healed by now. No, instead Jesus is right next to me, suffering with me, and whispering words of encouragement and love to me."

In the Body of Christ nothing is wasted, everything has its place, even depression.

St. Benedict Joseph Labre

Europe was teeming with beggars on the eve of the French Revolution and history recalls few of these faceless, nameless people. Still, one has not been forgotten: Benedict Joseph Labre, canonized in 1883. Born in Amettes, France, on March 27, 1748, Benedict was the son of Jean Baptiste Labre and Anne Barbe Gransire. This eldest son of a farming family soon won the hearts of the neighboring villagers with his honesty, thoughtfulness, and notable intelligence. From his earliest years, Benedict was set apart for the priesthood, and he actually spent ten years studying under the tutelage of his uncles, who were also priests. Benedict desired to be ordained to the priesthood, but as time went on he did not feel attracted by the life of a parish priest. Instead, Benedict desired a stricter monastic lifestyle, a longing that grew as he read the sermons of Père Le Jeune, a fiery sixteenth-century Oratorian preacher whose harsh interpretation of Scripture and frightening depictions of judgment influenced Benedict's natural inclination to mortification. As he read and re-read Le Jeune's sermons, Benedict's salutary fear of sin grew into horror of being completely cut off from God. Eventually, painful scruples beset him that endured throughout this life.

Benedict began a life of harsh penitence in expiation for sins committed against the "good God." He also sought to join a monastery. He asked to be admitted to the Trappists, but was refused. He knocked at the door of the Carthusian monks, who also turned him down. At last, when he approached the Cistercians, he was accepted. Shortly after he experienced the joy of admittance to the novitiate of the Cistercian Abbey of Septfonts, the darkness that had been his constant companion from his youth returned.

"You and I don't know the process by which the human is transhumanised: what do we know of the kind of suffering they must undergo on the way of illumination?"

T.S. Eliot, *The Cocktail Party*

Benedict worked hard on the grounds surrounding the monastery. When he fell gravely ill with a fever, the monks worried about this young novice who wanted so much to spend his life in penance, but was more than strict with himself and suffered from scrupulosity and an exaggerated sense of guilt. The abbot finally had to tell Benedict that his health was not strong enough to endure the rigors of monastic life at the Abbey of Septfonts. God must have some other plan for him.

Benedict felt crushed at not being able to fulfill his life's dream. He had no desire to return home, so he resolved to find his "cloister" in the world.

In 1770, Benedict began a pilgrimage, crisscrossing Europe and praying at shrines in Germany, Italy,

France, Switzerland, and Spain. He traveled about as a homeless beggar, ridiculed by many and reverenced by others who noticed the many hours he spent in prayer and in works of charity for those poorer than himself. He traveled from shrine to shrine for seven years, spending entire days in prayer at any church he came across. In truth, he lived a life more rigorous than that of a cloister, exposed to all kinds of weather, suffering the hardship of the homeless. In 1777, he settled down in Rome, sleeping in the Coliseum and praying daily in the churches of the city. As he grew weaker with age and illness, he moved into shelters for the poor. On Good Friday, 1783, after the services for the Veneration of the Cross at the Sanctuary of the Madonna dei Monti, Benedict collapsed on the street and died. Benedict had told his confessor only seven days before that he was finally free of scruples, of sorrow, of every shred of his miserable sense of unworthiness. An entire life of wandering and struggle, humiliation and searching had at last opened up onto a horizon of love that left him filled with joy.

The sufferings that people embrace with God often borrow or take on some of God's immensity and mystery. People suffering from depression or other psychological illnesses are invited by God to achieve more than mere "productive living." Usefulness, productivity, appearances, and motivation are but the surface of all that life can be. Those "sidelined" by depression have the possibility of being the prophetic voices of the divine to a world mesmerized by efficiency and immediacy.

This is not easy. Like Benedict, you may know only the anguished struggle. You may feel useless in comparison to your former capacity for work. You may know nothing of saints and prophets whose lives were far from easy. You may even distance yourself from God. It does not matter. Christ creates a sculpture of your life, using the illnesses of body as well as sufferings of the mind to chisel the richest details. While depression may affect your dreams and lifestyle, the intensity of your spirit's yearning transforms darkness into light.

Countless health care professionals, counselors, priests, lay ministers, friends, family members have felt blessed to witness this slow, painful, but marvelous transformation. Mildred Duff, co-founder of The Guild of St. Benedict Joseph Labre,[7] which offers spiritual support for the emotionally troubled and the mentally ill, their family and friends, writes some 100 letters a month to people who have shared with her their struggles and their sufferings. Through these letters, Mildred glimpses the amazing work of God in the lives of those who suffer from depression. In response to one woman's anguish, Mildred wrote words that can encourage and sustain all of us on our journey.

> If words were only hugs you would feel my loving arms around you right now. You must know and remember always that God and his Mother, who is also your mother, love you with a love that surpasses all others.

---

7. If you would like more information on The Guild of St. Benedict Joseph Labre, send a letter or request to P.O. Box 200, Buzzards Bay, MA 02532.

You are Mary's precious child who wears the crown of thorns, and your brother Jesus is suffering with you.

If these words seem too deep to understand right now, just know that Jesus knows what you are feeling now and listen to what Jesus is saying to you: "Others don't see me in you! But you must, for I am asking you: Will you wear the crown of thorns with me? Keep your heart and your head high for together you and I will offer our suffering to save even those who reject you and me...."

Yes, Benedict Joseph Labre will help you wear your "crown of thorns." Ask him for help.... Do the best you can under your circumstances. Just try!! That is what we ask our members to do and what I must do too. Just try!!"

Suggestion for prayer

My Good, my All, sole Object of my love—O come! I long for Thee, I sigh after Thee, I wait for Thee! Every little delay seems a thousand years! Come, Lord Jesus, and tarry not.

Prayer of St. Benedict Joseph Labre

⚘ ❀ ⚘
For one who is depressed

Read the life of St. Benedict Joseph Labre or St. Thérèse of Lisieux. Think about joining the Guild of St. Benedict.

For a friend:

Thank God for the way God is working in the life of your friend. Tell him or her that you have thanked God for his or her presence in your life.

Mother Teresa's "Dark Night"

Countless pictures of Mother Teresa reveal her warm smile. She was truly, as she so desired to be, an "apostle of joy," radiating an invincible faith. No one, except her spiritual directors, however, knew the darkness into which she had been plunged from 1947 to the end of her life. Feelings of doubt, loneliness and abandonment accompanied this darkness. Through visions and locutions Jesus had called her to leave the Sisters of Loreto and begin the Missionaries of Charity in India. This community of sisters would be Jesus' fire of love among the poorest of the poor. But from the moment she left the convent and began to walk the streets of Calcutta, the visions ceased, never to return. God seemed absent and heaven empty. She felt, along with so many of us, the terrible pain of loss, of God not wanting us, of God not being God, of God not really existing. According to Carol Zaleski, Mother Teresa suffered the classic dark night of the modern person: "radical doubt, doubting not only one's own state of grace, but God's promises and even God's existence."[8] As one

8. Carol Zaleski, "The Dark Night of Mother Teresa," *First Things,* May 2003, pp. 24–27.

of us, she shows us a path through the doubt and despair. Mother Teresa converted her feelings of abandonment *by* God into an act of abandonment *to* God.[9] In so doing, she bore witness to a fidelity for which the world is starving.[10]

The pain of darkness, doubt, and uncertainty became an integral part of her spirituality and vocation. The pain she suffered enabled her to enter into poverty much deeper than the misery she met on the streets of Calcutta. She came to know first hand the poverty of meaninglessness and loneliness that the depressed suffer. She could understand how difficult it is to believe, to hope for something better, and to trust that God has something beautiful in mind for us.

Mother Teresa's beautiful smile became her message to those suffering depression or doubt: "keep smiling." You need only resolve to love and to believe. It takes an act of the will, renewed daily, even hourly. Such a smile does not ride on the crest of surges of feelings. Mother Teresa's smile is truly an act of faith that depression and despair do not have the last word, not now, not ever. Depression has no power against the determination to believe.

9. Ibid.

10. Ibid.

Epilogue

Do you find yourself in the dark night of depression, this place of hopeless, stripping loneliness and meaninglessness? All hope and faith may seem truly extinguished. St. John of the Cross, who was imprisoned in complete darkness for nine months as a result of his beliefs, profoundly experienced this desolation and depression. He described the experience as the soul feeling itself to be impure and miserable, unworthy of God or any other creature. In mental suffering and depression, it may be nearly impossible for you to know how much of what you experience is mental illness and how much is the baffling experience of the dark night through which God leads those whom he loves. Fortunately, you do not need to sort that out.

Thankfully, depression is no more a period of complete loss than the winter season. The place where you are can open up and become new life. It is a creative time, even if you do not perceive it as such. The saints you have met in this book and the key moments in the history of salvation have shown that vital actions can be accomplished even in weakness. God does not need our strength; God prefers to work with weakness. God himself became weak. In our humbled spirit, God's creative Spirit is freer to work in us. Spiritual author Maria Boulding once said, "Like the bare trees, it may be that we allow the glory to shine through at these times more purely than in our summer prosperity."[11] God seems to prefer this pattern. From Abraham, who walked into an uncertain future on the word of a God he did not know, to Jesus, crucified in weakness and failure, it becomes clear that God works in no other way.

Through weakness, something new breaks into our world. Through you, something new is born for the rest of us who hurry briskly by. *You* have a vocation that the world needs. As John Paul II wrote in his Apostolic Letter, *On the Christian Meaning of Human Suffering:*

Suffering cannot be transformed and changed by a grace from outside, but from within.... However, this interior process does not always follow the same pattern.... Christ does not answer directly and he does not answer in the abstract this human questioning about the meaning of suffering. Man hears Christ's saving answer as he himself gradually becomes a sharer in the sufferings of Christ. The answer which comes through this sharing...is above all a call: Follow me! Come! Take part through your suffering in this work of saving the world, a salvation achieved through my suffering! Through my cross.[12]

---

11. Maria Boulding, *The Coming of God* (Collegeville: Liturgical Press, 1986), p. 41.

12. John Paul II, *On the Christian Meaning of Human Suffering* (Boston: Pauline Books and Media, 1984), n. 26.

In your suffering, you become a great prophet by
bearing Christ's cross with his strength and in his light.

ᏮᎷᏮᏞᏮᏮᏮᏞᏮᏮ

Immersed in the ever Creative Power
that penetrates my private world
in rhythms sure and confident,
I open to the mysterious Presence
that silently weaves people and events,
forever overlapping lives and times,
giving rise to indelible impression
upon the spatial memory
and we, travelers of current history,
evoke in one another
a need for response and belonging
in the world we call our lives.
No one without another,
no man without his past,
vital exchange of intimacies
impress a heart forever.
Today is the unfolding mystery
that bespeaks eternal motion,
whose purpose, beyond the stars,
defies finite contingency.

Sr. Thomas Halpin, FSP
June 8, 1994

Kathryn James Hermes, FSP is a member of the Congre-gation of the Daughters of St. Paul. She directs their Electronic Publishing Department at Pauline Books & Media, and is the author of *Beginning Contemplative Prayer: Out of Chaos, Into Quiet; Close Your Eyes to See; Prayers for Surviving Depression; The Journey Within: Prayer as a Path to God* and co-author of *The Rosary: Contemplating the Face of Christ.* She has an M.T.S. from Weston Jesuit School of Theology.

BOOKS & MEDIA

The Daughters of St. Paul operate book and media centers at the following addresses. Visit, call or write the one nearest you today, or find us on the World Wide Web, www.pauline.org

CALIFORNIA

3908 Sepulveda Blvd, Culver City, CA 90230	310-397-8676
2640 Broadway Street, Redwood City, CA 94063	650-369-4230
5945 Balboa Avenue, San Diego, CA 92111	858-565-9181

FLORIDA

145 S.W. 107th Avenue, Miami, FL 33174	305-559-6715

HAWAII

1143 Bishop Street, Honolulu, HI 96813	808-521-2731
Neighbor Islands call:	866-521-2731

ILLINOIS

172 North Michigan Avenue, Chicago, IL 60601	312-346-4228

LOUISIANA

4403 Veterans Memorial Blvd, Metairie, LA 70006	504-887-7631

MASSACHUSETTS

885 Providence Hwy, Dedham, MA 02026	781-326-5385

MISSOURI

9804 Watson Road, St. Louis, MO 63126	314-965-3512

NEW JERSEY

561 U.S. Route 1, Wick Plaza, Edison, NJ 08817	732-572-1200

NEW YORK

150 East 52nd Street, New York, NY 10022	212-754-1110

PENNSYLVANIA

9171-A Roosevelt Blvd, Philadelphia, PA 19114	215-676-9494

SOUTH CAROLINA

243 King Street, Charleston, SC 29401	843-577-0175

TENNESSEE

4811 Poplar Avenue, Memphis, TN 38117	901-761-2987

TEXAS

114 Main Plaza, San Antonio, TX 78205	210-224-8101

VIRGINIA

1025 King Street, Alexandria, VA 22314	703-549-3806

CANADA

3022 Dufferin Street, Toronto, ON M6B 3T5	416-781-9131